July 2nd 2002.

To: Maree + Keith

Congratulations on your 'China'
Wedding Anniversary.

Enjoy cooking some yummy
Oriental delights!

From: Ivan + Gerry xo

quick and easy
chinese
& oriental cooking

In this book you will find a wide range of Chinese and Oriental-inspired recipes for every occasion and taste. A traditional Chinese meal would consist of two parts – the 'fan' or the staple grain in the form or rice, noodles or dumplings and the 'cai' which is the rest of the meal and includes the fish, meat, poultry and vegetable dishes. A typical meal would contain a soup, one fan dish and three or four cai dishes. When planning a Chinese meal choose a variety of cooking techniques. This makes it easier for you as the cook and more interesting for those eating the meal. This old Chinese proverb sums up how the Chinese feel about food: 'To the ruler, people are heaven; to the people, food is heaven.'

CONTENTS

THE PANTRY SHELF
Unless otherwise stated, the following ingredients used in this book are:

Cream	Double, suitable for whipping
Flour	White flour, plain or standard
Sugar	White sugar

WHAT'S IN A TABLESPOON?
NEW ZEALAND
1 tablespoon = 15 mL or 3 teaspoons
UNITED KINGDOM
1 tablespoon = 15 mL or 3 teaspoons
AUSTRALIA
1 tablespoon = 20 mL or 4 teaspoons
The recipes in this book were tested in Australia where a 20 mL tablespoon is standard. All measures are level.

The tablespoon in the New Zealand and the United Kingdom sets of measuring spoons is 15 mL. In many recipes this difference will not matter. For recipes using baking powder, gelatine, bicarbonate of soda, small quantities of flour and cornflour, simply add another teaspoon for each tablespoon specified.

SOUPS

*Soups are an important part of Chinese and Asian
cuisine and are eaten at any time of the day. In many Asian
countries a bowl of chicken and rice soup is a popular breakfast,
noodle and vegetable broths are quick lunch meals and soup is
served at the end of a formal Chinese banquet.*

Oriental Seafood Soup

Fish and Coriander
Soup

Japanese Pork Soup

Beef and Tomato
Soup

Oriental Seafood Soup

Oriental Seafood Soup

4 large dried Chinese mushrooms
60 g/2 oz vermicelli noodles
6 cups/1.5 litres/2^1/2 pt chicken stock
500 g/1 lb firm white fish fillets,
cut into strips
60 g/2 oz ham, cut into strips
1 tablespoon soy sauce
250 g/8 oz cooked prawns, shelled
and deveined
4 spring onions, chopped
4 large spinach leaves, shredded

1   Place mushrooms in a bowl and cover with boiling water. Set aside to soak for 20 minutes or until mushrooms are tender. Drain, remove stalks if necessary and chop mushrooms.

2   Cook noodles in boiling water in a large saucepan following packet directions. Drain and set aside.

3   Place stock in a large saucepan and bring to the boil. Reduce heat, add fish, ham and soy sauce and simmer for 2-3 minutes or until fish is just cooked. Stir in mushrooms, prawns, spring onions and spinach and cook for 2-3 minutes longer or until heated through.

4   To serve, place noodles in a large serving bowl, pour over soup and serve immediately.

Serves 4

Fish and Coriander Soup

250 g/8 oz firm white fish fillets, cut
into 2.5 cm pieces
1 tablespoon cornflour
4 cups/1 litre/1^3/4 pt chicken stock
2 teaspoons grated fresh ginger
2 teaspoons soy sauce
2 tablespoons cider vinegar
2 tablespoons chopped fresh coriander

1   Toss fish pieces in cornflour and set aside.

2   Place stock, ginger, soy sauce and vinegar in a large saucepan and bring to the boil. Reduce heat, add fish and simmer for 2-3 minutes or until fish is just cooked. Stir in coriander and serve immediately.

Serves 4

Chicken stock is the basis of many Chinese soups. For a more traditional flavour you might like to make a Chinese chicken stock. To make stock, you will need 1 chicken; 2 carrots, roughly chopped; 2 onions, roughly chopped; 4 stalks celery, chopped; 2.5 cm/1 in piece fresh ginger, peeled; and 2 teaspoons soy sauce. Cut chicken into pieces, place in a large saucepan, add water and bring to the boil. Reduce heat, cover and simmer for 1^1/2 hours, skimming fat from the surface as it rises. Remove chicken from pan and discard. Add vegetables and ginger to pan, cover and simmer for 15 minutes. Stir in soy sauce and simmer for 5 minutes longer. Strain stock, refrigerate, then remove fat from top of stock. Use immediately or freeze until required.

Japanese Pork Soup

JAPANESE PORK SOUP

Dashi is the basic Japanese fish stock that gives many Japanese dishes their characteristic flavour. It is available in an instant form and today most Japanese cooks would use the instant dashi in the same way as Western cooks use stock cubes. Instant dashi is available from Asian food stores.

1 onion, very thinly sliced
6 cups/1.5 litres/2¹/₂ pt chicken stock
315 g/10 oz pork fillet, thinly sliced
250 g/8 oz canned bamboo shoots, drained
2 tablespoons liquid dashi (optional)
1 tablespoon grated fresh ginger
4 spring onions, sliced
1 small carrot, cut into thin strips

1 Place onion and chicken stock in a large saucepan and bring to the boil. Reduce heat, cover and simmer for 10 minutes.

2 Add pork, bamboo shoots, dashi (if using), ginger and spring onions, cover and simmer for 5-6 minutes or until pork is tender. Stir in carrot strips and serve immediately.

Serves 6

Beef and Tomato Soup

125 g/4 oz fillet steak, thinly sliced and
cut into strips
1 tablespoon dry sherry
2 teaspoons soy sauce
2 teaspoons cornflour
1 tablespoon oil
6 cups/1.5 litres/2^1/$_2$ pt chicken stock
2 tomatoes, peeled and chopped
2 eggs, beaten
2 spring onions, sliced

1   Place meat, sherry, soy sauce and
cornflour in a bowl and mix to combine.
Cover and set aside to stand at room
temperature for 20 minutes.

2   Heat oil in a wok or large saucepan,
add meat mixture and stir-fry for 2-3
minutes or until meat browns. Remove
meat from pan and set aside.

3   Add stock and tomatoes to pan, bring
to the boil and boil for 3-4 minutes or
until tomatoes are just cooked. Stir beaten
egg into stock mixture.

4   Place meat in serving bowls, spoon
over soup, sprinkle with spring onions and
serve immediately.

As a rule of thumb the light,
delicate soups would
accompany a meal, while
the heavier, more hearty
soups are served on their
own as a light meal.

Beef and Tomato Soup

Serves 4

SNACKS

*Eating little and often is a characteristic of people
from Asian countries; finger foods and snacks are very
popular. In this chapter you will find recipes for favourite
snacks such as Fried Porkballs, Beef Satay and Steamed
Pork Wontons. The foods in this chapter also make
great starters for Asian meals.*

Spring Rolls

SPRING ROLLS

12 spring roll or wonton wrappers, each
12.5 cm/5 in square
vegetable oil for deep-frying

PORK AND VEGETABLE FILLING
125 g/4 oz lean pork mince
30 g/1 oz bean sprouts
1/4 small cabbage, chopped
2 spring onions, chopped
1 tablespoon cornflour
1 tablespoon soy sauce
1 teaspoon sesame oil

1   To make filling, place pork, bean sprouts, cabbage, spring onions, cornflour, soy sauce and sesame oil in a bowl and mix to combine.

2   Place a tablespoon of filling in the centre of each wrapper, fold one corner over filling, then tuck in the sides and roll up, sealing with water.

3   Heat vegetable oil in a large saucepan until a cube of bread browns in 50 seconds and cook a few Spring Rolls at a time for 3-4 minutes or until golden. Drain on absorbent kitchen paper and serve immediately.

Makes 12

Wonton or spring roll wrappers are available frozen from Asian food shops and some supermarkets.

SAN CHOY BOW

1 tablespoon vegetable oil
500 g/1 lb lean pork mince
1 tablespoon cornflour
3/4 cup/185 mL/6 fl oz water
1 tablespoon dry sherry
1/2 teaspoon sesame oil
1 tablespoon oyster sauce
2 small fresh red chillies, chopped
1 clove garlic, crushed
1 teaspoon grated fresh ginger
220 g/7 oz canned water chestnuts,
drained and chopped
12 lettuce leaves

1   Heat oil in a large wok or frying pan, add mince and stir-fry for 4-5 minutes or until browned. Remove from pan and drain on absorbent kitchen paper. Wipe pan clean.

2   Place cornflour, water, sherry, sesame oil and oyster sauce in a bowl, mix to combine and set aside. Return mince to pan, add chillies, garlic, ginger, water chestnuts and cornflour mixture and cook over a high heat, stirring constantly, for 4-5 minutes or until mixture boils and thickens and pork is cooked.

3   Spoon hot pork mixture into lettuce leaves and serve immediately.

Makes 12

You might like to serve these as they do in restaurants. Serve the meat and lettuce leaves separately and allow each person to assemble their own. This not only prevents the lettuce from becoming soggy but is also fun. To fully enjoy this dish it must be eaten in your fingers.

THAI MEATBALLS AND FISHBALLS

Rice wine is used extensively in Asian cooking. It is made from glutinous rice, yeast and water and is available from Asian food stores. If it is unavailable, dry sherry is a suitable substitute.

5 cups/1.2 litres/2 pt chicken stock

MEATBALLS
3 dried Chinese mushrooms
500 g/1 lb lean beef mince
1 tablespoon chopped fresh coriander
3 spring onions, chopped
1 tablespoon rice wine or dry sherry
freshly ground black pepper

FISHBALLS
100 g/3^1/$_2$ oz canned shrimps, drained
750 g/1^1/$_2$ lb firm white fish fillets
1 teaspoon grated fresh ginger
3 teaspoons cornflour

GINGER SAUCE
2 teaspoons chopped fresh ginger
2 tablespoons rice wine or dry sherry
2 tablespoons tamari (Japanese soy sauce)

1 To make Meatballs, place mushrooms in a bowl, cover with boiling water and set aside to soak for 20 minutes or until mushrooms are tender. Drain, remove stalks if necessary and chop mushrooms.

2 Place mushrooms, beef, coriander, spring onions, rice wine or sherry and black pepper to taste in a bowl and mix well to combine. Using wet hands, form mixture into 18 balls and set aside.

3 To make Fishballs, place shrimps and fish in a food processor and process to chop finely. Transfer fish mixture to a bowl, add ginger and cornflour and mix well to combine. Using wet hands, form mixture into 18 balls and set aside.

4 To make sauce, place ginger, rice wine or sherry and tamari (Japanese soy sauce) in a small bowl and mix to combine.

5 Place stock in a large saucepan, bring to the boil and cook 5-6 meatballs or fishballs at a time for 4-5 minutes or until cooked through. Serve immediately with sauce.

Serves 6

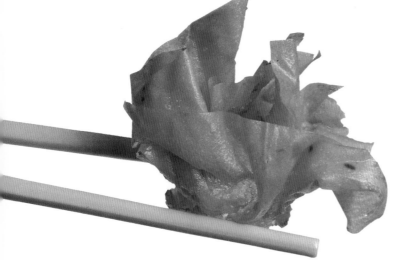

From top: Thai Meatballs and Fishballs, Wafer-wrapped Prawns, Seafood Tempura

WAFER-WRAPPED PRAWNS

375 g/12 oz cooked prawns, shelled,
deveined and coarsely chopped
1 fresh green chilli, seeded and chopped
2 teaspoons oyster sauce
24 spring roll or wonton wrappers, each
12.5 cm/5 in square
vegetable oil for deep-frying

CHILLI SAUCE
4 tablespoons tomato sauce
1-2 teaspoons chilli sauce
water
1/2 teaspoon sesame oil

1   Place prawns, chilli and oyster sauce in a bowl and mix well to combine.

2   Place a heaped teaspoon of prawn mixture in the centre of each wrapper, then draw the corners together and twist them to form small bundles.

3   To make sauce, place tomato sauce, chilli sauce, water and sesame oil in a small saucepan. Cook over a medium heat, stirring constantly, for 3-4 minutes or until heated through.

4   Heat vegetable oil in a large saucepan until a cube of bread browns in 50 seconds. Cook a few bundles at a time for 3-4 minutes or until golden. Drain on absorbent kitchen paper. Serve immediately with Chilli Sauce.

Makes 24

Oyster sauce is made from a concentrate of cooked oysters, soy sauce and brine. It is a thick brown sauce with a rich flavour and is used not only in cooking but also as a condiment.

SEAFOOD TEMPURA

vegetable oil for deep-frying
500 g/1 lb firm white fish fillets, cut
into strips
250 g/8 oz salmon fillet, cut into strips
250 g/8 oz uncooked prawns, shelled
and deveined, tails left intact
90 g/3 oz calamari (squid) rings
chilli or soy sauce for dipping

BATTER
2 eggs
1 cup/250 mL/8 fl oz iced water
1 cup/125 g/4 oz flour

1   To make batter, place eggs and water in a bowl and beat until frothy. Add flour, beat until blended, then place bowl over ice.

2   Heat oil in a large wok or saucepan until a cube of bread browns in 50 seconds. Dip fish strips in batter and cook a few at a time for 3-4 minutes or until golden. Repeat with salmon, prawns and calamari (squid). Serve immediately with chilli or soy sauce.

Serves 6

The secret to a good tempura batter is that it is freshly made and cold. For best results the batter should be made just prior to cooking.
You might like to make vegetable tempura, in which case use a selection of vegetables. Popular vegetables for tempura include red or green pepper strips, snow peas (mangetout), asparagus, cauliflower and broccoli.

BEEF SATAY

500 g/1 lb lean rump steak,
cut into 1 cm/^{1}/$_2$ in cubes
2 cloves garlic, crushed
60 g/2 oz almonds, finely chopped
1 tablespoon chilli sauce
1 tablespoon brown sugar

PEANUT SAUCE
2 teaspoons chilli sauce
4 tablespoons crunchy peanut butter
^{1}/$_3$ cup/90 mL/3 fl oz water
3 tablespoons fruit chutney

1   Place meat, garlic, almonds, chilli sauce and sugar in a bowl and mix to combine. Cover and set aside to stand for 30 minutes or in the refrigerator overnight.

2   To make sauce, place chilli sauce, peanut butter, water and chutney in a small saucepan and cook over a low heat, stirring, for 5 minutes or until heated through and ingredients are combined.

3   Thread meat onto 12 bamboo skewers and cook under a preheated grill for 4-5 minutes each side or until meat is tender and cooked to your liking.

Makes 12 skewers

Satay can be made using any meat and this recipe is just as delicious made with pork, lamb or chicken instead of the beef.

STEAMED PORK WONTONS

2 dried Chinese mushrooms
185 g/6 oz lean pork mince
1 tablespoon chopped canned
bamboo shoots
2 tablespoons finely chopped celery
1 spring onion, finely chopped
1 clove garlic, crushed
1 tablespoon soy sauce
1 tablespoon dry sherry
1 teaspoon sugar
36 wonton or spring roll wrappers,
each 12.5 cm/5 in square

1   Place mushrooms in a bowl, cover with boiling water and set aside to soak for 20 minutes or until mushrooms are tender. Drain, remove stalks if necessary and chop mushrooms.

2   Place mushrooms, pork, bamboo shoots, celery, spring onion, garlic, soy sauce, sherry and sugar in a bowl and mix well to combine. Cover and refrigerate for 30 minutes or until ready to cook wontons.

3   Place a teaspoon of pork mixture in the centre of each wrapper, brush edges with water, draw wrapper up around mixture and pinch together. Place wontons in a bamboo steamer set over a saucepan of simmering water, cover and cook for 6 minutes or until wontons are cooked through.

Makes 36

The most useful size bamboo steamer for home cooking is 25 cm/10 in in diameter. The steamer is designed so that several can be stacked one on top of another and so multiple cooking can take place. The food that takes the longest to cook is placed in the bottom steamer with the food requiring the shortest cooking time in the top steamer. Bamboo steamers are available from Asian food shops.

FRIED PORKBALLS

500 g/1 lb lean pork mince
30 g/1 oz rice noodles, broken, soaked
and well-drained
1 small onion, finely chopped
1 clove garlic, crushed
1 teaspoon grated fresh ginger
1 teaspoon finely chopped fresh lemon
grass or 1 teaspoon finely grated
lemon rind
$^1/_4$ teaspoon ground turmeric
freshly ground black pepper
flour
vegetable oil for deep-frying

1   Place pork and noodles in a bowl and mix to combine.

2   Place onion, garlic, ginger and lemon grass or lemon rind in a food processor or blender and process to make a paste. Add onion mixture, turmeric and black pepper to taste to meat mixture and mix well to combine.

3   Form meat mixture into 24 balls, dust with flour, place on a plate lined with plastic food wrap, cover and refrigerate until required. Heat oil in a large wok or saucepan until a cube of bread browns in 50 seconds. Cook balls a few at a time for 3-4 minutes or until golden and cooked through. Drain on absorbent kitchen paper and serve immediately.

If mixture appears a little dry add a little water; if too moist add a little cornflour.

Fried Porkballs

Makes 24

Deep-fried Wontons

250 g/8 oz lean pork mince
2 teaspoons soy sauce
185 g/6 oz frozen spinach, thawed and
excess water squeezed out
freshly ground black pepper
36 wonton or spring roll wrappers,
each 12.5 cm/5 in square
vegetable oil for deep-frying

Lean beef or chicken mince
can be used in place of the
pork mince if you wish.

1   Place pork, soy sauce, spinach and
black pepper to taste in a bowl and mix
well to combine.

2   Place a teaspoon of pork mixture in
the centre of each wrapper, brush edges
with water, draw wrapper up around
mixture and pinch together.

3   Heat oil in a large wok or saucepan
until a cube of bread browns in 50
seconds. Cook wontons a few at a time
for 3-4 minutes or until golden and
cooked through. Drain on absorbent
kitchen paper and serve immediately.

Makes 36

Egg Rolls

vegetable oil for deep-frying

PRAWN AND PORK FILLING
1 tablespoon peanut (groundnut) oil
125 g/4 oz uncooked prawns, shelled,
deveined and chopped
185 g/6 oz lean pork mince
2 leeks, cut into thin strips
60 g/2 oz bean sprouts
1 tablespoon finely chopped celery
1 clove garlic
1 tablespoon soy sauce
2-3 drops Tabasco sauce

PANCAKES
2 cups/250 g/8 oz flour
4 eggs
3/4 cup/185 mL/6 fl oz water

Egg rolls are popular
throughout Asia with each
country having its own
version. You can vary the
filling to suit your own taste
and according to what is
available.

1   To make filling, heat peanut
(groundnut) oil in a large wok or frying
pan, add prawns, pork, leeks, bean sprouts,
celery and garlic and stir-fry for 3 minutes.
Add soy and Tabasco sauces and simmer,
stirring frequently, for 10 minutes.
Remove meat mixture from pan and
set aside.

2   To make pancakes, place flour, eggs
and water in a bowl and beat until
smooth. Pour 2-3 tablespoons batter into
a lightly greased frying pan and cook over
a medium heat for 3-4 minutes or until
top of pancake is dry. Slide cooked
pancake onto a plate. Repeat with
remaining mixture to make 8-12
pancakes.

3   Place a spoonful of filling in the centre
of each pancake, fold in the sides and
gently roll up to form a parcel.

4   Heat oil in a large wok or frying pan
until a cube of bread browns in 50
seconds. Cook 3-4 parcels at a time for
5-7 minutes or until golden and crisp
and heated through. Drain on absorbent
kitchen paper. Cut each roll into three
and serve immediately.

*Makes 8-12, depending on size of
pancakes*

SESAME PRAWN BALLS

1 kg/2 lb uncooked prawns, shelled
and deveined
1 onion, chopped
$^1/_2$ teaspoon garam masala
$^1/_4$ teaspoon ground turmeric
1 cup/185 g/6 oz ground rice
1 teaspoon sesame oil
2 tablespoons finely chopped
fresh coriander
3 tablespoons sesame seeds
vegetable oil for deep-frying

1   Place prawns, onion, garam masala
and turmeric in a food processor and
process until smooth. Transfer prawn
mixture to a bowl, add ground rice,
sesame oil and coriander and mix well to
combine. Cover and refrigerate for at
least 1 hour.

2   Using wet hands, roll mixture into
small balls, then roll in sesame seeds.
Place balls on a plate lined with plastic
food wrap and refrigerate for 30 minutes.

3   Heat oil in a large wok or saucepan
until a cube of bread browns in 50
seconds. Cook 5-6 balls at a time for
4-5 minutes or until golden and heated
through. Drain on absorbent kitchen
paper and serve immediately.

Serves 6

In Asia a wok would usually
be used for deep-frying,
however it is probably easier
and safer to use a deep fat
fryer or a deep-sided
saucepan.

Sesame Prawn Balls

SEAFOOD

Fish and seafood are popular ingredients in Chinese cooking. To the Chinese, freshness is everything, so the less time that elapses between catching the fish and eating it the better. The most popular way of cooking fish is to leave it whole, as this preserves the flavour and keeps it moist.

Chilli Ginger Crab

Fish in Chilli Bean
Sauce

Seafood Combination

Egg Foo Yung

Thai Garlic Prawns

Prawn Chow Mein

Fried Chilli Prawns

Steamed Fish

Seafood and Noodle
Stir-Fry

Steamed Fish Parcels

Chilli Ginger Crab

14

CHILLI GINGER CRAB

4 crabs
2 teaspoons peanut (groundnut) oil
2 onions, sliced
1^1/$_2$ cups/375 mL/12 fl oz chicken stock
1 tablespoon soy sauce
1 tablespoon chilli sauce
2 tablespoons dry sherry
2 cloves garlic, crushed
1 tablespoon grated fresh ginger
4 spring onions, cut into
3 cm/1^1/$_4$ in lengths

1 Cut crabs in half and remove gills and stomach sac from underside.

2 Heat oil in a large wok or frying pan, add onions and stir-fry for 3-4 minutes or until soft. Add crabs and stir-fry for 3 minutes.

3 Add stock, soy sauce, chilli sauce, sherry, garlic, ginger and spring onions to pan, cover and cook for 5 minutes or until crabs change colour and are cooked. Serve immediately.

Serves 4

To the Chinese, serving fish or seafood is a sign of prosperity.

FISH IN CHILLI BEAN SAUCE

500 g/1 lb firm white fish fillets, cut into 5 cm/2 in wide strips
3 tablespoons cornflour
3 tablespoons peanut (groundnut) oil
2 spring onions, sliced diagonally into 5 cm/2 in lengths
1 clove garlic, finely chopped
1 teaspoon finely chopped fresh ginger

CHILLI BEAN SAUCE
^{1}/$_4$ cup/60 mL/2 fl oz chicken stock
2 teaspoons yellow bean sauce
^{1}/$_4$ teaspoon chilli powder or to taste
1 tablespoon dry sherry
2 teaspoons soy sauce
1 teaspoon sesame oil

1 Toss fish strips in cornflour and set aside.

2 To make sauce, place stock, bean sauce, chilli powder, sherry, soy sauce and sesame oil in a small bowl and mix to combine. Set aside.

3 Heat peanut (groundnut) oil in a wok or large frying pan, add fish and stir-fry for 4-5 minutes or until golden and cooked through. Remove fish from pan, drain on absorbent kitchen paper and set aside.

4 Drain all but 1 tablespoon oil from pan, add spring onions, garlic and ginger and stir-fry for 30 seconds. Add sauce and bring to the boil. Reduce heat, return fish to pan and cook, stirring frequently, for 2 minutes or until heated through. Serve immediately.

Serves 4

Yellow bean sauce is a thick, spicy sauce made from yellow beans, flour and salt. It has a distinctive flavour and is available from Asian food shops. There are two varieties: whole yellow bean sauce or crushed yellow bean sauce. The whole yellow bean sauce is less salty and has a better texture.

SEAFOOD COMBINATION

¹/4 cup/60 mL/2 fl oz vegetable oil
375 g/12 oz uncooked large prawns,
shelled and deveined
250 g/8 oz calamari (squid) rings
250 g/8 oz firm white fish fillets, cut
into cubes
125 g/4 oz scallops
1 red pepper, cut into strips
250 g/8 oz snow peas (mangetout)
220 g/7 oz canned sliced bamboo
shoots, drained
2 cloves garlic, crushed
2 teaspoons grated fresh ginger
2 teaspoons cornflour
¹/2 cup/125 mL/4 fl oz chicken stock
1 teaspoon sesame oil
2 teaspoons soy sauce

Serves 4

1   Heat 2 tablespoons vegetable oil in a
wok or frying pan, add prawns, calamari
(squid), fish and scallops and stir-fry for
2-3 minutes. Remove seafood from pan
and set aside.

2   Add remaining vegetable oil to pan,
heat and add red pepper, snow peas
(mangetout), bamboo shoots, garlic and
ginger and stir-fry for 4-5 minutes or until
red pepper and snow peas (mangetout)
are tender.

3   Combine cornflour, chicken stock,
sesame oil and soy sauce and stir into pan.
Cook, stirring constantly, until sauce
boils and thickens. Return seafood to pan
and cook for 2-3 minutes or until heated
through. Serve immediately.

With their quick cooking
times, fish and seafood are
perfect for stir-frying.

EGG FOO YUNG

500 g/1 lb uncooked prawns, shelled
and deveined
1 egg white, lightly beaten
1 teaspoon cornflour
2 eggs
1 teaspoon sesame oil
¹/4 cup/60 mL/2 fl oz chicken stock
2 teaspoons dry sherry
2 teaspoons soy sauce
2 tablespoons vegetable oil
3 spring onions, finely chopped

Serves 2

1   Place prawns, egg white and cornflour
in a bowl and mix to combine. Cover and
refrigerate for 20 minutes.

2   Place eggs, sesame oil, stock, sherry
and soy sauce in a bowl and whisk to
combine.

3   Heat 1 tablespoon vegetable oil in a
wok or frying pan, add prawns and stir-fry
for 2-3 minutes or until prawns just
change colour. Remove prawns from pan
and set aside. Wipe pan clean.

4   Heat remaining oil in pan, add egg
mixture and stir-fry for 1 minute or until
egg just begins to set. Return prawns to
pan and stir-fry for 1 minute longer.
Sprinkle with spring onions and serve
immediately.

This dish is also delicious
made with crab meat or fish
or you might like to try
minced pork or beef in place
of the prawns. A vegetarian
version using asparagus and
snow peas (mangetout) is
also delicious.

THAI GARLIC PRAWNS

6 cloves garlic, crushed
6 tablespoons chopped fresh coriander
3 tablespoons vegetable oil
500 g/1 lb uncooked large prawns, shelled and deveined, tails left intact
$^3/_4$ cup/185 mL/6 fl oz water
$^1/_4$ cup/60 mL/2 fl oz fish sauce
1 tablespoon sugar
freshly ground black pepper

1   Place garlic, coriander and 2 tablespoons oil in a food processor or blender and process until smooth.

2   Heat remaining oil in a large wok or frying pan, add garlic mixture and stir-fry for 2 minutes. Add prawns and stir-fry to coat with garlic mixture. Stir in water, fish sauce, sugar and black pepper to taste and stir-fry until prawns are cooked.

Fish sauce is an essential ingredient in the cuisines of Thailand, Vietnam, the Philippines and southern China. It is made from salted fish or prawns and is a thin brown liquid with a salty taste.

Thai Garlic Prawns

Serves 4

PRAWN CHOW MEIN

250 g/8 oz dried egg noodles
1 kg/2 lb uncooked prawns, shelled,
deveined and roughly chopped
2 teaspoons dry sherry
1 tablespoon soy sauce
1 tablespoon peanut (groundnut) oil
1 clove garlic, crushed
60 g/2 oz snow peas (mangetout)
2 rashers bacon, chopped
$1/2$ teaspoon sugar
2 spring onions, chopped
1 teaspoon sesame oil

Chow Mein means 'stir-fried'
noodles. In this recipe the
main ingredient is prawns but
Chow Mein can be made
with almost anything that you
like. Leftover Chow Mein is
delicious served cold as a
salad.

1   Cook noodles in boiling water in a
large saucepan following packet
directions. Drain and place in cold water
until ready to use.

2   Place prawns, sherry and 2 teaspoons
soy sauce in a bowl and toss to combine.
Cover and set aside to marinate for 15
minutes.

3   Heat 2 teaspoons peanut (groundnut)
oil in a wok or large frying pan, add
prawns and stir-fry for 2 minutes or until
prawns just change colour. Remove
prawns from pan and set aside. Wipe pan
clean.

4   Drain noodles, place on absorbent
kitchen paper and pat dry. Heat
remaining peanut (groundnut) oil in pan,
add garlic, snow peas (mangetout) and
bacon and stir-fry for 2-3 minutes or until
snow peas (mangetout) just change colour
and bacon is cooked. Add noodles, sugar,
spring onions and remaining soy sauce
and stir-fry for 2 minutes, then add prawns
and stir-fry for 2 minutes longer or until
heated through. Stir in sesame oil and
serve immediately.

Serves 4

FRIED CHILLI PRAWNS

1 kg/2 lb uncooked prawns,
heads only removed
2 teaspoons finely chopped fresh ginger
1 tablespoon dry sherry
1 tablespoon cornflour
vegetable oil for deep-frying
1 teaspoon salt
1 teaspoon chilli sauce or to taste

In this recipe, only the heads
are removed from the
prawns before deep-frying.

1   Place prawns, ginger, sherry and
cornflour in a bowl and mix to combine.
Cover and refrigerate for 20 minutes.

2   Heat oil in a wok or large saucepan
until a cube of bread browns in 50
seconds. Drain prawns and cook a few at
a time for 1 minute or until prawns
change colour.

3   Remove prawns from pan. Drain off
oil and discard. Heat pan, add prawns,
salt and chilli sauce and stir-fry for 1
minute. Serve immediately.

Serves 4

STEAMED FISH

2 small whole fish, such as snapper or
bream
1 tablespoon finely chopped fresh ginger
1 tablespoon soy sauce
1 teaspoon sugar
1 tablespoon white vinegar
2 rashers bacon, cut into strips
1 small carrot, cut into thin strips
4 spring onions, cut into
3 cm/1¼ in lengths

1   Place fish in a shallow glass or ceramic dish. Combine ginger, soy sauce, sugar and vinegar. Pour soy mixture over fish, cover and set aside to marinate for 30 minutes.

2   Line a bamboo steamer with nonstick baking paper. Place fish in steamer, pour over marinade and sprinkle with bacon, carrot and spring onions.

3   Cover steamer, place over a wok of simmering water and steam for 10-15 minutes or until fish flakes when tested with a fork.

Steamed Fish

Serves 2

The Chinese always serve whole fish with the head pointing towards the guest of honour. It is believed that this assures him or her of good fortune.

SEAFOOD AND NOODLE STIR-FRY

375 g/12 oz egg noodles
250 g/8 oz calamari (squid) hoods
250 g/8 oz asparagus, cut diagonally into
5 cm/2 in pieces
2 tablespoons peanut (groundnut) oil
1 clove garlic, crushed
2 small fresh red chillies, finely chopped
1 teaspoon finely grated fresh ginger
500 g/1 lb uncooked large prawns,
shelled and deveined, tails left intact
250 g/8 oz scallops
$^1/_2$ red pepper, sliced
60 g/2 oz snow peas (mangetout), sliced
diagonally into 5 cm/2 in pieces
2 tablespoons sesame seeds, toasted

SAUCE
1 tablespoon cornflour
1 tablespoon sugar
3 tablespoons tomato sauce
1 teaspoon oyster sauce
1 tablespoon soy sauce
1 teaspoon sesame oil
1 cup/250 mL/8 fl oz water

1 Cook noodles in a large saucepan of
boiling water following packet
instructions. Drain, then rinse under hot
water. Spread out on absorbent kitchen
paper.

2 Cut calamari (squid) hoods along one
side and spread out flat with inside facing
up. Using a sharp knife mark a diamond
pattern over the surface, then cut into
diamond-shaped pieces. Set aside.

3 Boil, steam or microwave asparagus
until it just changes colour. Drain and
rinse under cold running water. Set aside.

4 Heat peanut (groundnut) oil in a wok
or frying pan, add garlic, chillies and
ginger and stir-fry for 1 minute. Add
calamari (squid), prawns, scallops, red
pepper, snow peas (mangetout) and
asparagus and stir-fry for 2-3 minutes or
until prawns just change colour. Add
noodles to pan and stir-fry for 1-2 minutes
longer.

5 To make sauce, place cornflour, sugar,
tomato sauce, oyster sauce, soy sauce,
sesame oil and water in a small bowl and
whisk to combine. Pour sauce into pan
and heat for 2-3 minutes longer or until it
boils and thickens. Sprinkle with sesame
seeds and serve immediately.

Serves 4

This recipe is another version
of a seafood Chow Mein.

STEAMED FISH PARCELS

6 x 90 g/3 oz firm white fish fillets
¹/₂ teaspoon ground saffron
1 onion, chopped
2 cloves garlic, sliced
2 teaspoons sliced fresh ginger
1 small fresh red chilli, seeded
and chopped
1 tablespoon cornflour
³/₄ cup/185 mL/6 fl oz coconut milk
1 teaspoon sesame oil
1 stalk fresh lemon grass, chopped or
2 teaspoons finely grated lemon rind
6 large lettuce leaves

1   Rub fish fillets with saffron.

2   Place onion, garlic, ginger, chilli, cornflour, coconut milk, sesame oil and lemon grass or lemon rind in a food processor or blender and process until smooth.

3   Steam or microwave lettuce leaves until just soft. Drain and pat dry with absorbent kitchen paper. Place a fish fillet in the centre of each lettuce leaf and spoon over a little of the coconut milk mixture. Fold lettuce leaves around fish fillets to form neat parcels.

4   Cut six foil squares large enough to enclose fish parcels. Place a parcel on each foil square and fold to enclose. Place parcels in a bamboo steamer set over a saucepan of simmering water and steam for 20 minutes or until fish flakes when tested with a fork.

Serves 6

Before using a bamboo steamer for the first time, wash it well then place it over a saucepan of simmering water and steam it, empty, for about 5 minutes.

POULTRY

All types of birds are used in Chinese cooking but chicken is the most popular and highly regarded. As with fish, the fresher the bird the better and in Asian countries chicken would usually be bought live. To impress a special guest, a Chinese hostess is likely to announce that she has killed a chicken in his or her honour.

Stir-fried Chicken with Cashews

22

STIR-FRIED CHICKEN WITH CASHEWS

2 tablespoons vegetable oil
1 red onion, cut into wedges, separated
1 carrot, sliced diagonally
1 clove garlic, crushed
1 teaspoon grated fresh ginger
375 g/12 oz boneless chicken breast
fillets, cut into strips
1 head broccoli, cut into florets
60 g/2 oz unsalted cashews
$^1/_2$ cup/125 mL/4 fl oz chicken stock
2 teaspoons cornflour
2 teaspoons soy sauce
1 tablespoon dry sherry
$^1/_4$ teaspoon sesame oil
3 spring onions, sliced diagonally

1 Heat 1 tablespoon vegetable oil in a wok or frying pan, add onion, carrot, garlic and ginger and stir-fry for 5 minutes. Remove vegetable mixture and set aside.

2 Cook chicken in batches in pan for 2-3 minutes or until lightly browned. Remove and set aside.

3 Heat remaining vegetable oil in pan, add broccoli and cashews and stir-fry until broccoli just changes colour and cashews are golden.

4 Combine stock, cornflour, soy sauce, sherry and sesame oil. Return vegetables and chicken to pan, add cornflour mixture and cook, stirring, for 3-4 minutes or until sauce boils and thickens. Stir in spring onions.

Serves 4

Stir-frying is one of the most popular methods of Chinese cooking. A wok is best for stir-frying but a large frying pan can be used. As stir-frying is so quick it's important that you have all your ingredients prepared before you start cooking.

SPICED DUCK

4 cups/1 litre/1$^3/_4$ pt chicken stock
$^1/_2$ cup/125 mL/4 fl oz soy sauce
2 teaspoons finely chopped fresh ginger
2 cloves garlic, finely chopped
2 teaspoons five spice powder
1 x 2 kg/4 lb duck
vegetable oil for deep-frying

CHILLI MARINADE
2 tablespoons sugar
2 tablespoons dry sherry
$^1/_2$ teaspoon five spice powder
$^1/_2$ teaspoon sesame oil
1 tablespoon soy sauce
1 teaspoon chilli sauce

1 Place stock, soy sauce, ginger, garlic and five spice powder in a large saucepan, cover and bring to the boil. Add duck, bring back to the boil and boil for 1 minute. Remove pan from heat and set aside to stand, covered, until liquid cools to room temperature.

2 To make marinade, place sugar, sherry, five spice powder, sesame oil, soy sauce and chilli sauce in a bowl and mix well to combine.

3 Remove duck from liquid and drain well. Cut duck in half through the breast and back bones and pat dry. Place duck, cut side down on a baking tray. Rub skin with marinade and set aside to marinate for 2 hours.

4 Heat oil in a large saucepan and cook half a duck at a time for 10 minutes or until golden brown and cooked through. Drain on absorbent kitchen paper.

Serves 4

The Chinese believe that duck is a symbol of wholesomeness and fidelity.

To serve, using a knife or cleaver cut each half duck into serving-sized pieces.

INDONESIAN CHICKEN

3 tablespoons vegetable oil
4 boneless chicken breast fillets,
cut into 2 cm/³/4 in cubes
250 g/8 oz green beans, cut into
2.5 cm/1 in pieces
¹/4 cup/60 mL/2 fl oz lemon juice
2 tablespoons soy sauce
1 tablespoon brown sugar
2 teaspoons ground turmeric
¹/2 cup/125 mL/4 fl oz water

1   Heat oil in a wok or frying pan, add chicken and stir-fry for 3-4 minutes or until chicken browns. Remove chicken from pan and set aside.

2   Add beans to pan and stir-fry for 2 minutes. Stir in lemon juice, soy sauce, sugar, turmeric and water, bring to the boil and simmer for 3-5 minutes or until sauce reduces and thickens slightly. Return chicken to pan and cook for 2-3 minutes longer or until chicken is cooked through.

Serves 4

LEMON CHICKEN

6 dried Chinese mushrooms
1 teaspoon salt
freshly ground black pepper
5 tablespoons peanut (groundnut) oil
2 kg/4 lb chicken thigh fillets, cut into
bite-sized pieces
1 green pepper, chopped
1 teaspoon finely chopped fresh ginger
2 tablespoons finely grated lemon rind
4 spring onions, sliced
3 tablespoons dry sherry
2 tablespoons soy sauce
1 teaspoon cornflour
1 tablespoon water
1 tablespoon lemon juice

1   Place mushrooms in a bowl, cover with boiling water and set aside to soak for 20 minutes or until mushrooms are tender. Drain, remove stalks if necessary and chop mushrooms.

2   Mix salt, black pepper to taste and 1 tablespoon oil to a paste. Place chicken in a bowl, add salt and pepper paste and mix well to coat chicken. Heat 3 tablespoons oil in a wok or frying pan, add chicken and cook for 10 minutes or until chicken is just cooked. Remove chicken from pan, set aside and keep warm.

3   Heat remaining oil in pan, add mushrooms, green pepper, ginger, lemon rind and spring onions. Stir in sherry and soy sauce and bring to the boil. Combine cornflour and water and stir into sauce. Return chicken to pan and cook for 5 minutes longer or until chicken is heated through. Stir in lemon juice and serve immediately.

Serves 6

For successful stir-frying, heat your wok until very hot, then add the oil. Swirl the wok to coat the surface and continue to heat until the oil is almost smoking before adding the food. Following this procedure will ensure that the food does not stick to the wok. An exception to this is when the first ingredients to be added to the wok are garlic, spring onions, ginger or chillies. Add these ingredients immediately after adding the oil or they will burn.

Lemon Chicken is delicious served with steamed rice and steamed or stir-fried broccoli.

Easy Peking Duck

Oven temperature
180°C, 350°F, Gas 4

1 x 2.5 kg/5 lb duck
6 cups/1.5 litres/2¹/₂ pt water
2 teaspoons chopped fresh ginger
3 tablespoons brown sugar
3 spring onions, roughly chopped
1 cucumber, peeled, seeded and cut
into 5 cm/2 in strips

BARBECUE SAUCE
2 tablespoons hoisin sauce
1 tablespoon water
¹/₂ teaspoon sesame oil
1 teaspoon brown sugar

PANCAKES
1 cup/125 g/4 oz flour
1 cup/250 mL/8 fl oz boiling water
1 tablespoon sesame oil

1   Rinse duck inside and out, then pat
dry with absorbent kitchen paper. Place
duck in front of a fan and leave to dry for
1 hour.

2   Place water in a large saucepan and
bring to the boil. Add ginger, sugar and
spring onions, then carefully lower duck
into boiling water, making sure that the
whole duck is covered. Remove duck
immediately and discard liquid. Place
duck in front of fan again and leave to
dry for 1 hour.

3   To make sauce, place hoisin sauce,
water, sesame oil and sugar in a small
saucepan, bring to the boil and cook,
stirring, for 30 seconds. Remove pan
from heat and set aside to cool.

4   Place duck on a roasting rack set in a
baking dish and bake for 30 minutes.
Reduce oven temperature to 150°C/
300°F/Gas 2 and bake for 1 hour longer.
Then increase oven temperature to
200°C/400°F/Gas 6 and bake until the
skin of the duck is brown and crispy.

5   To make pancakes, sift flour into a
large bowl, then stir in boiling water and
sesame oil and mix well. Knead dough to
a smooth mass and set aside to stand for
30 minutes. Shape dough into a roll and
cut into approximately 16 pieces. Roll out
each piece into a 10 cm/4 in circle and fry
without fat in a nonstick frying pan until
little bubbles appear on the surface, then
turn over and cook other side. Set aside
and keep warm until ready to serve.

6   To serve, remove all crispy skin from
duck and cut into 4 x 6 cm/1¹/₂ x 2¹/₂ in
pieces. Cut breast meat of duck into
similar size pieces and arrange skin, meat,
pancakes and cucumber on a serving
platter. Transfer sauce to a serving bowl
and serve with duck. To eat, spread a
pancake with a teaspoon of sauce, top
with a piece of skin, a piece of meat and a
piece of cucumber. Roll up pancake and
eat in your fingers.

Serves 4

This somewhat simplified
method of preparing and
cooking Peking Duck is still
time-consuming but is worth
the effort for a special dinner
party.
Due to the length of time
that Peking Duck takes to
prepare, most restaurants
that serve it require that you
order it at least a day in
advance. In China preparing
and cooking Peking Duck is
considered an art form.

Smoked Chicken

SMOKED CHICKEN

$^1\!/_2$ cup/125 g/4 oz sugar
3 tablespoons tea leaves
2 tablespoons salt
1 x 1.5 kg/3 lb chicken
freshly ground black pepper
1 tablespoon soy sauce
2 teaspoons sesame oil

1   Line a baking dish with sheets of aluminium foil large enough to completely enclose the chicken. Combine sugar, tea leaves and salt and spread out over foil. Place a roasting rack in the baking dish and place chicken on rack. Sprinkle chicken liberally with black pepper, bring foil up around chicken to completely enclose and bake for 1 hour.

2   Combine soy sauce and sesame oil. Open foil parcel, brush chicken with soy sauce mixture and bake, uncovered, for 20 minutes longer or until chicken is cooked through. To serve, cut into pieces and serve immediately.

Serves 6

Oven temperature
190°C, 375°F, Gas 5

Chicken cooked in this way is moist with a crisp skin and distinctive flavour.

27

BRAISED GINGER CHICKEN

2 tablespoons vegetable oil
500 g/1 lb boneless chicken breast
fillets, cut into strips
1 red pepper, cut into rings
1 green pepper, cut into rings
1 onion, cut into eighths
2 cloves garlic, crushed
2 teaspoons grated fresh ginger
1 tablespoon cornflour
1 tablespoon sherry
2 teaspoons soy sauce
1¼ cups/315 mL/10 fl oz chicken stock

1   Heat oil in a wok or frying pan and stir-fry chicken in batches for 3-4 minutes or until brown. Remove chicken from pan and set aside.

2   Add red and green peppers, onion, garlic and ginger and stir-fry for 4-5 minutes or until peppers and onion are soft. Combine cornflour, sherry, soy sauce and stock. Return chicken to pan and stir in cornflour mixture. Cook, stirring constantly, for 2-3 minutes or until mixture boils and thickens and chicken is heated through. Serve immediately.

Serves 4

Fresh ginger is an important ingredient in Asian cooking. To store fresh ginger, peel and place in a glass jar. Cover with sherry, store in the refrigerator and use as you would fresh ginger. Ginger stored in this way will keep for many months. The sherry left after the ginger is used can be used in cooking.

SPICY THAI CHICKEN

2 tablespoons vegetable oil
1-2 teaspoons curry paste
1 clove garlic, crushed
1 fresh red chilli, finely chopped
6 spring onions, chopped
500 g/1 lb boneless chicken breast
fillets, skinned and minced
440 g/14 oz canned tomatoes, undrained
and mashed
3 tablespoons chopped fresh basil

1   Heat oil in a wok or frying pan, add curry paste, garlic, chilli and spring onions and stir-fry for 2 minutes. Add chicken mince and stir-fry for 3-4 minutes or until chicken is brown.

2   Stir in tomatoes and basil, bring to the boil, reduce heat and simmer, uncovered, for 8-10 minutes or until most of the liquid has evaporated.

Serves 4

When handling fresh chillies do not put your hands near your eyes or allow them to touch your lips. To avoid discomfort and burning, wear rubber gloves. Freshly minced chilli is available in jars from supermarkets.

Right: Po Chero
Far right: Chicken Stir-Fry

Po Chero

8 large Chinese dried mushrooms
2 tablespoons peanut (groundnut) oil
4 chicken drumsticks
375 g/12 oz pork fillets, cubed
4 Chinese sausages, cut into pieces
2 onions, sliced
2 cloves garlic, crushed
250 g/8 oz sweet potato, diced
315 g/10 oz canned chickpeas, drained
2 cups/500 mL/16 fl oz chicken stock
2 tablespoons tomato paste (purée)
1 tablespoon soy sauce
1 tablespoon cornflour
2 tablespoons water
1/4 Chinese cabbage, roughly chopped

Chinese sausages are highly
flavoured sausages made
with chopped lean and fat
pork and spices. They are
available from Asian food
stores.

1   Place mushrooms in a bowl, cover
with boiling water and set aside to soak for
20 minutes or until mushrooms are
tender. Drain, remove stalks if necessary
and cut mushrooms in half.

2   Heat oil in a large frying pan, add
chicken and cook, turning frequently
until brown on all sides. Remove chicken
from pan and set aside. Cook pork and
sausages in the same way.

3   Return chicken, pork and sausages to
pan, add mushrooms, onions, garlic, sweet
potato and chickpeas and mix to
combine. Combine stock, tomato paste
(purée) and soy sauce, add to pan, cover
and cook over a low heat for 30 minutes
or until meat and vegetables are cooked
through and tender.

4   Combine cornflour and water. Stir
cabbage and cornflour mixture into meat
and vegetable mixture and cook, stirring
constantly, until sauce boils and thickens.
Serve immediately.

Serves 4

CHICKEN STIR-FRY

1 tablespoon peanut (groundnut) oil
500 g/1 lb boneless chicken breast
fillets, cut into strips
1 red pepper, cut into strips
1 small head broccoli, broken
into florets
2 small zucchini (courgettes), chopped
1 carrot, chopped
2 teaspoons cornflour blended
with 1 tablespoon water
2 teaspoons grated fresh ginger
1 tablespoon honey
2 tablespoons soy sauce
1 teaspoon chilli sauce, or to taste
1 tablespoon hoisin sauce

1   Heat oil in a wok or large frying pan,
add chicken and stir-fry for 3-4 minutes or
until just cooked. Remove chicken from
pan and set aside.

2   Add red pepper, broccoli, zucchini
(courgettes) and carrot to pan and stir-fry
for 2-3 minutes or until vegetables are just
tender.

3   Stir in cornflour mixture, ginger,
honey, soy sauce, chilli sauce and hoisin
sauce and cook, stirring constantly, for 2-3
minutes or until sauce boils and thickens.

4   Return chicken to pan and stir-fry for
2-3 minutes or until chicken is heated
through. Serve immediately.

Serves 4

Peanut (groundnut) oil with
its pleasant, mild taste is the
preferred oil for Chinese
cooking.

MEAT

*When the Chinese talk about meat they inevitably
mean pork. While beef, lamb and goat are used in Chinese
cooking they are not as popular as pork, but they are more com-
mon in northern China. In many of the recipes that call for pork
you can substitute with beef if you wish.*

PORK WITH NOODLES

315 g/10 oz pork fillet, sliced
1 tablespoon soy sauce
155 g/5 oz rice noodles
2 tablespoons peanut (groundnut) oil
$^1/_2$ onion, sliced
1 green pepper, chopped
$^1/_2$ cauliflower, broken into florets
2 tablespoons water
$^1/_2$ teaspoon chilli sauce

1   Place pork and soy sauce in a bowl and toss to combine.

2   Soak noodles in hot water for 15 minutes or until soft. Drain and set aside.

3   Heat 1 tablespoon oil in a wok or frying pan, add pork and stir-fry for 2 minutes. Remove pork from pan and set aside. Add remaining oil, onion, green pepper and cauliflower and stir-fry for 2 minutes. Add water, cover pan and simmer for 5 minutes or until cauliflower is just tender.

4   Return pork to pan, add noodles and chilli sauce and stir-fry for 2-3 minutes or until heated through. Serve immediately.

Serves 4

Rice noodles are available dry from Asian food stores and some supermarkets. They are white in colour and come in a variety of shapes.

CHINESE ROAST BEEF

1.5 kg/3 lb beef eye fillet

GINGER MARINADE
2 tablespoons soy sauce
2 tablespoons dry sherry
4 cloves garlic, finely chopped
1 teaspoon grated fresh ginger
2 teaspoons brown sugar

DIPPING SAUCE
3 tablespoons chilli sauce
3 tablespoons plum sauce

1   Tie beef to form an even shape and place in a shallow glass or ceramic dish.

2   To make marinade, place soy sauce, sherry, garlic, ginger and sugar in a small bowl and whisk to combine. Pour marinade over meat and turn to coat. Cover and set aside to marinate at room temperature for 3 hours or in the refrigerator overnight.

3   If marinated overnight, bring beef to room temperature, drain, reserve marinade and place beef in a baking dish. Brush beef with marinade and bake for 20 minutes, basting with additional marinade after 10 minutes. Remove beef from oven, cover and set aside to stand for 10 minutes.

4   To serve, slice beef and accompany with chilli and plum sauces for dipping.

Oven temperature
240°C, 475°F, Gas 8

When planning a Chinese or Asian-style meal, try to choose dishes that use a variety of cooking methods and ingredients. In this way you will have not only a combination of textures and flavours but you will also find cooking and serving easier.

Pork with Noodles

Serves 6

BEEF IN BEAN SAUCE

1 tablespoon vegetable oil
1 clove garlic, crushed
1 tablespoon grated fresh ginger
1 onion, finely sliced
350 g/11 oz lean rump steak,
cut into strips
2 teaspoons sesame oil
$^1/_2$ red pepper, sliced
90 g/3 oz bean sprouts
60 g/2 oz snow peas (mangetout)
$1^1/_2$ tablespoons black bean sauce
1 tablespoon soy sauce
$^1/_4$ cup/60 mL/2 fl oz beef stock
1 teaspoon sugar
1 teaspoon cornflour blended
with 1 tablespoon water

1   Heat vegetable oil in a wok or frying pan, add garlic and ginger and stir-fry for 1 minute. Add onion and beef and stir-fry for 3 minutes or until beef is browned. Remove meat mixture from pan and set aside.

2   Heat sesame oil in pan, add red pepper, bean sprouts and snow peas (mangetout) and stir-fry for 1 minute. Add black bean sauce, soy sauce, stock, sugar and cornflour mixture and cook, stirring, until mixture thickens slightly. Return meat mixture to pan and cook for 2-3 minutes longer or until heated through.

Serves 4

Black beans are small black soy beans which are preserved by fermenting with salt and spices. They should be rinsed well before using. Any leftover beans and liquid will keep indefinitely in a sealed jar in the refrigerator.

Left: Beef in Bean Sauce
Below: Stir-fried Barbecued Pork

STIR-FRIED BARBECUED PORK

10 dried Chinese mushrooms
350 g/11 oz rice noodles
1 tablespoon sesame oil
250 g/8 oz Chinese barbecued pork,
cut into thin strips
1 tablespoon grated fresh ginger
1 red, green or yellow pepper, cut
into strips
125 g/4 oz snow peas (mangetout)
60 g/2 oz canned bamboo shoots,
drained and sliced
2 tablespoons honey
$^1/_4$ cup/60 mL/2 fl oz soy sauce
1 tablespoon red wine vinegar

1   Place mushrooms in a bowl, cover
with boiling water and set aside to soak
for 20 minutes or until mushrooms are
tender. Drain, remove stalks if necessary
and slice mushrooms.

2   Cook noodles in boiling water
following packet directions. Drain, set
aside and keep warm.

3   Heat oil in a wok or frying pan, add
pork, ginger and mushrooms and stir-fry
for 2 minutes. Add red, green or yellow
pepper, snow peas (mangetout) and
bamboo shoots, and stir-fry for 1 minute
longer. Remove pork and vegetable
mixture from pan, set aside and keep
warm.

4   Add honey, soy sauce and vinegar to
pan and cook, stirring, until mixture boils.
Add noodles and toss to coat with honey
mixture. Serve noodles topped with pork
and vegetable mixture.

Serves 4

Chinese barbecued pork is
available from Asian food
stores. If it is unavailable you
can use cold roast pork
instead.

Right: Lamb with Bamboo Shoots
Below: Beef with Spinach

BEEF WITH SPINACH

2 tablespoons peanut (groundnut) oil
500 g/1 lb lean rump steak,
cut into strips
1 bunch/500 g/1 lb spinach, leaves
removed and shredded
2 teaspoons grated fresh ginger
2 cloves garlic, crushed
3 teaspoons cornflour
1 cup/250 mL/8 fl oz water
2 tablespoons satay sauce
2 tablespoons dry sherry
1 tablespoon soy sauce
60 g/2 oz roasted cashew nuts

1 Heat oil in a wok or frying pan, add steak and stir-fry for 3-4 minutes or until browned. Remove meat from pan and drain on absorbent kitchen paper.

2 Add spinach, ginger and garlic to pan and stir-fry for 2-3 minutes or until spinach starts to wilt. Combine cornflour, water, satay sauce, sherry and soy sauce, stir into spinach mixture and cook for 2-3 minutes or until mixture boils and thickens.

3 Return meat to pan, add cashew nuts and cook for 2-3 minutes or until heated through.

Serves 4

When buying a wok, choose a large one – with at least a 35 cm/14 in in diameter and deep sides. A heavy wok made of carbon steel is better than a light stainless steel or aluminium one. Remember it is easier to cook a small amount of food in a large wok than to cook a large amount of food in a small wok!

LAMB WITH BAMBOO SHOOTS

2 tablespoons vegetable oil
4 lean lamb leg chops, trimmed of all
visible fat
8 spring onions, chopped
2 cloves garlic, crushed
1 cup/250 mL/8 fl oz beef stock
1 tablespoon soy sauce
1 teaspoon chilli paste (sambal oelek)
$^1/4$ cup/60 mL/2 fl oz white wine
1 teaspoon five spice powder
125 g/4 oz canned bamboo shoots,
drained and sliced
250 g/8 oz rice noodles

1   Heat 1 tablespoon oil in a large frying pan, add chops and cook for 2-3 minutes on each side or until browned. Transfer chops to a large saucepan. Add three-quarters of the spring onions and garlic to frying pan and stir-fry for 2 minutes, then add to saucepan with chops.

2   Add stock, soy sauce, chilli paste (sambal oelek), wine and five spice powder to chops, bring to the boil, reduce heat, cover and simmer for 1 hour or until lamb is tender. Remove chops from cooking liquid, set aside to cool, then shred meat. Drain cooking liquid and discard solids.

3   Heat remaining oil in frying pan, add remaining spring onions and stir-fry for 2 minutes. Add shredded lamb and bamboo shoots and stir-fry for 1 minute longer.

4   Cook noodles in boiling water following packet directions, drain, spoon meat mixture over noodles and serve immediately.

Serves 4

Chopsticks are the eating utensils used in many, but not all, Asian countries. Special long chopsticks are also used for cooking, stirring, beating and whipping.

INDONESIAN PORK

2 tablespoons vegetable oil
500 g/1 lb lean diced pork
1 cup/250 mL/8 fl oz coconut milk

CHILLI PASTE
8 fresh red chillies, seeded and chopped
4 cloves garlic, chopped
2 onions, chopped
1 tablespoon chopped fresh ginger
1 teaspoon chopped fresh lemon grass or
1 teaspoon finely grated lemon rind
1 teaspoon tamarind pulp (optional)
$^1/_2$ teaspoon dried shrimp paste,
crumbled

1 To make paste, place chillies, garlic, onions, ginger, lemon grass or lemon rind, tamarind (if using) and shrimp paste in a food processor or blender and process to make a smooth paste.

2 Heat oil in a large saucepan, add chilli paste and cook over a low heat, stirring occasionally, for 5 minutes. Add pork and cook to brown all sides. Stir in coconut milk and simmer, stirring constantly, for 20 minutes or until sauce thickens and meat is tender.

Serves 4

Tamarind is the large pod of the tamarind, or Indian date, tree. After picking, it is seeded and peeled then pressed into a dark brown pulp. Tamarind is available from Asian food shops.

ORIENTAL LAMB

500 g/1 lb lean lamb leg steaks, cut
into thin strips
2 tablespoons oyster sauce
2 tablespoons dry white wine
1 teaspoon sugar
$^1/_2$ teaspoon sesame oil
2 tablespoons vegetable oil
1 bunch/500 g/1 lb spinach, leaves
removed and cut into large pieces, stalks
cut into 2.5 cm/1 in pieces
2 teaspoons grated fresh ginger
$^1/_2$ teaspoon cornflour blended with
$^1/_4$ cup/60 mL/2 fl oz chicken stock

1   Place lamb, oyster sauce, wine, sugar
and sesame oil in a bowl and toss to
combine. Cover and set aside to marinate
for 20 minutes.

2   Heat oil in a wok or frying pan, add
lamb mixture and stir-fry in batches for
2-3 minutes or until meat browns.
Remove meat from pan and set aside.

3   Add spinach stalks and ginger to pan
and stir-fry for 3 minutes or until stalks
are just tender. Return meat to pan, add
spinach leaves and cornflour mixture and
cook, stirring constantly, for 3-4 minutes
or until spinach leaves start to wilt. Serve
immediately.

Serves 4

Sesame oil is used as a
flavouring, but not usually for
cooking. It has a strong
distinctive flavour and only a
small quantity is required. In
cooked dishes sesame oil is
usually added just prior to
serving. It will keep
indefinitely.

RED PEPPERED BEEF

500 g/1 lb lean rump steak, cut
into thin strips
2 teaspoons cornflour
4 tablespoons soy sauce
3 tablespoons vegetable oil
2 red peppers, cut into thin strips
1 small fresh red chilli, finely chopped
3 spring onions, cut into
5 cm/2 in lengths
1 clove garlic, crushed
2 teaspoons grated fresh ginger
1 teaspoon sugar
2 tablespoons dry sherry

1   Place meat in a bowl, sprinkle with
cornflour and 2 tablespoons soy sauce, toss
to combine and set aside to stand for 5
minutes.

2   Heat 1 tablespoon oil in a wok or
frying pan, add red peppers, chilli, spring
onions, garlic and ginger and stir-fry for
2-3 minutes. Remove vegetable mixture
from pan and set aside.

3   Heat remaining oil in pan, add meat
and stir-fry for 2-3 minutes or until
browned. Combine remaining soy sauce,
sugar and sherry. Return vegetable
mixture to pan, pour in soy sauce mixture
and cook, stirring, for 1 minute longer or
until heated through.

There are two types or wok
available: the Cantonese
wok and the pau wok. The
Cantonese wok has a
handle on either side while
the pau has just one long
handle. The Cantonese wok
is better for steaming and
deep-frying, while the pau
wok is best for stir-frying.

Indonesian Pork

Serves 4

SIMMERED BEEF

1.5 kg/3 lb piece topside
2 tablespoons peanut (groundnut) oil
1 clove garlic, crushed
2 teaspoons finely chopped fresh ginger
$^1/_2$ cup/125 mL/4 fl oz soy sauce
$^1/_3$ cup/90 mL/3 fl oz dry sherry
2 cups/500 mL/16 fl oz water
1 teaspoon five spice powder

1   Tie meat to form a neat shape and so that it holds its shape during cooking.

2   Heat oil in a wok or large saucepan, add meat and cook to brown on all sides. Add garlic, ginger, soy sauce, sherry, water and five spice powder to pan and bring to the boil. Cover, reduce heat and simmer, turning meat every 30 minutes for $1^1/_2$ hours or until meat is tender.

3   To serve, remove string, slice meat and spoon over sauce.

Serves 6

HONEY PORK

Oven temperature
180°C, 350°F, Gas 4

500 g/1 lb pork fillets
1 tablespoon tomato sauce
2 tablespoons honey
$^1/_4$ teaspoon five spice powder
2 teaspoons soy sauce
1 large head broccoli, broken into florets

SHERRY SAUCE
2 teaspoons cornflour
$^1/_2$ cup/125 mL/4 fl oz chicken stock
1 tablespoon dry sherry
1 teaspoon sugar
$^1/_2$ teaspoon oyster sauce

1   Place pork fillets in a shallow glass or ceramic dish. Place tomato sauce, 1 tablespoon honey, five spice powder and soy sauce in a small bowl, mix to combine, pour over pork, cover and set aside to marinate for 1 hour.

2   Drain pork, place in a baking dish and bake for 20 minutes. Brush fillets with remaining honey and bake for 10 minutes longer.

3   Boil, steam or microwave broccoli until just tender.

4   To make sauce, place cornflour, stock, sherry, sugar and oyster sauce in a small saucepan and cook over a medium heat, stirring, until sauce boils and thickens.

5   To serve, cut pork in thick slices and arrange on a serving platter. Surround with broccoli and spoon over sauce.

Serves 4

Five spice powder is a favourite ingredient in Chinese cooking. It adds a subtle anise flavour to Oriental dishes.

Honey Pork

PORK WITH CUCUMBER

The only time that you should ever need to scrub your wok is when it is new. The surface of a new wok is usually coated with an oil to protect it and this should be removed before using. To remove the oil, scrub it with a cream cleanser. Once the wok is cleaned it should be seasoned. To season a wok, heat it over a low heat, then add 2 tablespoons vegetable oil and rub this over the entire surface to lightly coat. Heat the wok over a low heat for 10-15 minutes, then wipe it with absorbent kitchen paper. Repeat this process until the paper you use to wipe the wok is clean.

315 g/10 oz lean diced pork
2 tablespoons soy sauce
1 teaspoon cornflour
2 tablespoons peanut (groundnut) oil
2 small cucumbers, diced
2 spring onions, sliced
1 teaspoon finely sliced fresh ginger
2 fresh red chillies, seeded and chopped

SESAME SAUCE
1 teaspoon sugar
2 teaspoons brown vinegar
1 tablespoon soy sauce
$^1/_2$ teaspoon cornflour
2 tablespoons water
1 tablespoon sesame oil

Serves 4

1   Place pork, soy sauce and cornflour in a bowl and mix to combine.

2   Heat oil in a wok or frying pan, add meat mixture and cucumbers and stir-fry for 3-4 minutes or until meat browns. Remove meat mixture from pan and set aside.

3   Add spring onions, ginger and chillies to pan and stir-fry for 1-2 minutes. Return pork mixture to pan and stir-fry for 5 minutes longer or until pork is cooked through.

4   To make sauce, combine sugar, vinegar, soy sauce, cornflour, water and sesame oil and stir into pan. Cook, stirring constantly, for 2-3 minutes or until sauce boils and thickens. Serve immediately.

Left: Pork with Cucumber
Below: Chinese Spareribs

CHINESE SPARERIBS

8 pork spareribs, trimmed of rind
and excess fat
$^1/_4$ cup/60 mL/2 fl oz dry sherry
2 tablespoons honey
2 tablespoons plum sauce
$^1/_4$ cup/60 mL/2 fl oz tomato sauce
2 fresh red chillies, seeded and chopped
2 cloves garlic, crushed
1 tablespoon grated fresh ginger
$^1/_2$ teaspoon five spice powder

1   Cut each sparerib into 3 pieces and place in a bowl. Combine sherry, honey, plum sauce, tomato sauce, chillies, garlic, ginger and five spice powder and pour over ribs. Mix well to coat ribs.

2   Place ribs and sauce mixture in a large frying pan, cover and cook over a low heat, stirring occasionally, for 1 hour or until pork is tender and glazed.

Serves 4

Plum sauce is available from Asian food shops and most supermarkets. Made from dried plums, apricots, vinegar, sugar and spices, it is a thick, sweet chutney-like sauce that is used as a condiment.

WARM THAI BEEF SALAD

1 kg/2 lb rump steak, cut into
2.5 cm/1 in thick steaks
1 cucumber, peeled and thinly sliced
fresh coriander leaves for garnishing
1 fresh red chilli, sliced

CORIANDER MARINADE
4 tablespoons soy sauce
2 tablespoons vegetable oil
1 teaspoon ground coriander
1 tablespoon finely chopped
fresh coriander
1 tablespoon brown sugar
freshly ground black pepper

1   Place steaks in a shallow glass or ceramic dish. To make marinade, place soy sauce, oil, ground and fresh coriander, sugar and black pepper to taste in a small bowl and mix to combine. Pour marinade over meat in dish, cover and set aside to marinate for at least 1 hour. Arrange overlapping cucumber slices on a large platter, cover and refrigerate until required.

2   Drain steaks and reserve marinade. Cook steaks under a preheated grill for 2-3 minutes each side or until cooked to your liking. Place reserved marinade in a small saucepan, bring to the boil and cook for 3-4 minutes. Thinly slice steaks, arrange slices on top of cucumber, spoon over marinade and garnish with coriander and sliced fresh chilli.

Traditionally the meat for this dish should be cooked rare.

Serves 8

Left: Sweet and Sour Pork
Far left: Warm Thai Beef Salad

SWEET AND SOUR PORK

2 egg yolks
1 tablespoon water
2 tablespoons cornflour
500 g/1 lb pork fillet, cut into
2 cm/^{3}/4 in cubes
vegetable oil for deep-frying

SWEET AND SOUR SAUCE
1 tablespoon vegetable oil
1 onion, cut into eighths
^{1}/2 red pepper, cut into cubes
^{1}/2 green pepper, cut into cubes
1 tablespoon cornflour
^{1}/2 cup/125 mL/4 fl oz water
2 tablespoons tomato sauce
2 teaspoons soy sauce
1 tablespoon white vinegar
350 g/11 oz canned pineapple pieces,
drained and juice reserved

Serves 4

1   Combine egg yolks and water. Place cornflour in a bowl and gradually stir in egg yolk mixture. Add pork and toss to coat.

2   Heat oil in a wok or large saucepan until a cube of bread browns in 50 seconds, and cook pork in batches for 7-10 minutes or until golden and cooked through. Remove pork and drain on absorbent kitchen paper.

3   To make sauce, heat oil in a wok or frying pan, add onion and red and green pepper and stir-fry for 5 minutes or until vegetables are soft. Combine cornflour, water, tomato sauce, soy sauce, vinegar and reserved pineapple juice and stir into pan. Cook, stirring constantly, for 2-3 minutes or until sauce boils and thickens.

4   Stir pork and pineapple pieces into sauce and cook for 3-4 minutes longer or until heated through. Serve immediately.

One of the most popular and undoubtedly famous Chinese recipes, Sweet and Sour Pork is delicious served with steamed or boiled rice and steamed Chinese cabbage.

CHOP SUEY

2 tablespoons vegetable oil
250 g/8 oz lean pork mince
$^1/_2$ Chinese cabbage, shredded
125 g/4 oz green beans, sliced diagonally
2 stalks celery, sliced diagonally
2 onions, chopped
1 carrot, chopped
1 cup/250 mL/8 fl oz chicken stock
2 teaspoons cornflour
1 tablespoon soy sauce
2 boneless chicken breast fillets, cooked and cut into cubes
250 g/8 oz uncooked prawns, shelled and deveined
250 g/8 oz canned bamboo shoots

1   Heat oil in a wok or large frying pan, add pork and stir-fry for 5 minutes or until browned.

2   Add cabbage, beans, celery, onions and carrot and stir-fry for 3-4 minutes. Place stock, cornflour and soy sauce in a small bowl and whisk to combine. Stir cornflour mixture into meat mixture and cook, stirring, for 3-4 minutes or until mixture boils and thickens.

3   Add chicken, prawns and bamboo shoots to pan and cook for 3-4 minutes longer or until prawns are cooked. Serve immediately.

Serves 6

Bamboo shoots, as the name suggests, are the young edible shoots of certain types of bamboo. They are pale yellow in colour and have a crunchy texture. Available canned you will find them in most Asian food shops and most supermarkets.

SPICED PORK FILLET

500 g/1 lb pork fillets
$^1/_2$ cup/125 mL/4 fl oz chicken stock
2 teaspoons cornflour

GINGER MARINADE
2 tablespoons hoisin sauce
1 tablespoon soy sauce
2 teaspoons vinegar
2 tablespoons dry sherry
1 teaspoon grated fresh ginger
2 tablespoons honey

1   Place pork fillets in a shallow glass or ceramic dish. To make marinade, place hoisin sauce, soy sauce, vinegar, sherry, ginger and honey in a small bowl, mix to combine. Pour marinade over pork, cover and set aside to marinate for 1 hour.

2   Drain pork and reserve marinade. Place pork in a baking dish and bake for 30 minutes, turning several times.

3   Place reserved marinade, stock and cornflour in a saucepan and cook, stirring, until sauce boils and thickens. To serve, slice pork and spoon sauce over slices.

Serves 4

Hoisin sauce, sometimes called Chinese barbecue sauce is a thick, brownish red sauce made from soy beans, vinegar, sugar, spices and other flavourings. It is used both in cooking and as a condiment.

Spiced Pork Fillet

PORK STIR-FRY

1 tablespoon vegetable oil
250 g/8 oz lean diced pork
1 clove garlic, crushed
2 tablespoons soy sauce
freshly ground black pepper
500 g/1 lb snake or green beans cut into
2 cm/³/4 in lengths
1 red pepper, cut into strips
6 spring onions, cut into
5 cm/2 in lengths
¹/2 teaspoon sesame oil
2 tablespoons toasted sesame seeds

1   Heat oil in a wok or frying pan, add pork and garlic and stir-fry for 3-4 minutes or until pork changes colour. Add soy sauce, black pepper to taste, beans and red pepper, and stir-fry for 2-3 minutes.

2   Reduce heat, cover pan and simmer for 20 minutes or until pork is tender. Stir in spring onions, sesame oil and sesame seeds and serve immediately.

Serves 4

The easiest way to toast a small quantity of sesame seeds is to place the seeds in a small frying pan and heat over a medium heat, shaking pan frequently, until seeds pop and are golden. Take care not to burn the seeds.

BEEF WITH BROCCOLI

500 g/1 lb lean rump steak, cut into
paper-thin slices
1 tablespoon soy sauce
1 tablespoon dry sherry
2 teaspoons grated fresh ginger
1 tablespoon vegetable oil
1 cup/250 mL/8 fl oz chicken stock
500 g/1 lb broccoli, broken into florets
2 teaspoons cornflour
2 teaspoons oyster sauce
2 teaspoons chilli sauce

1   Place meat, soy sauce, sherry and ginger in a bowl and mix to combine. Cover and set aside to stand for 30 minutes.

2   Heat oil in a wok or frying pan, add meat mixture and stir-fry for 4-5 minutes or until browned. Remove meat mixture from pan and set aside.

3   Add ¹/2 cup/125 mL/4 fl oz stock to pan and bring to the boil. Add broccoli to stock, cover and cook for 5 minutes or until broccoli is tender. Drain and reserve stock. Place broccoli around the edge of a serving platter, set aside and keep warm.

4   Combine cornflour, oyster sauce, chilli sauce and remaining stock, add to pan and bring to the boil. Return meat mixture to pan and cook, stirring, for 3-4 minutes or until heated through. Spoon meat mixture onto serving dish and serve immediately.

Serves 6

'To the ruler, people are heaven; to the people, food is heaven' – old Chinese proverb.

Pork Stir-Fry

BEEF AND NOODLES

250 g/8 oz egg noodles
1 tablespoon vegetable oil
500 g/1 lb lean rump steak,
cut into strips
1 onion, sliced
1 clove garlic, crushed
1/2 green pepper, cut into strips
1 teaspoon fish sauce
2 tablespoons sesame seeds, toasted
60 g/2 oz bean sprouts

1   Cook noodles in boiling water in a large saucepan following packet directions. Drain, set aside and keep warm.

2   Heat oil in a wok or frying pan, add beef and stir-fry for 3-4 minutes or until beef changes colour. Remove beef from pan and set aside. Add onion, garlic and green pepper to pan and stir-fry for 5 minutes or until onion is soft. Return beef to pan, add fish sauce, sesame seeds and bean sprouts and stir-fry for 2-3 minutes or until heated through. To serve, spoon beef mixture over noodles.

Serves 4

Egg noodles are available both fresh and dried. Flat noodles are usually used for soups while the rounded noodles are used for stir-frying. If Chinese egg noodles are unavailable, Italian egg noodles can be used instead.

PORK WITH MUSHROOMS

4 dried Chinese mushrooms
1 tablespoon vegetable oil
30 g/1 oz blanched almonds
250 g/8 oz lean pork mince
2 tablespoons soy sauce
2 teaspoons cornflour
1 teaspoon sugar
2 tablespoons water
freshly ground black pepper
1 tablespoon dry sherry
8 canned water chestnuts, drained
and finely chopped
60 g/2 oz fresh or frozen peas
2 stalks celery, diced
1 clove garlic, chopped
2 slices fresh ginger

1 Place mushrooms in a bowl, cover with boiling water and set aside to soak for 20 minutes or until mushrooms are tender. Drain and reserve liquid. Remove stalks from mushrooms if necessary and chop mushrooms finely.

2 Heat half the oil in a wok or frying pan, add almonds and stir-fry for 1-2 minutes or until golden. Remove and drain on absorbent kitchen paper, then chop finely.

3 Place pork, half the soy sauce, 1 teaspoon cornflour, sugar, water and black pepper to taste in a bowl and mix well to combine. In a separate bowl combine sherry, remaining soy sauce and cornflour, and reserved mushroom liquid.

4 Add remaining oil to pan and heat. Add water chestnuts, peas and celery, cover and cook for 2-3 minutes. Remove vegetable mixture and set aside. Add garlic, ginger and pork mixture to pan and stir-fry for 2 minutes. Reduce heat, cover and simmer for 5 minutes. Add vegetable mixture, pour in sherry mixture and cook, stirring constantly, until mixture boils and thickens. Sprinkle with almonds and serve immediately.

Serves 2

Water chestnuts are about the size of a walnut and are the edible tubers of the Chinese sedge (Chinese water chestnut). They are white in colour and crunchy in texture and readily available canned. Before using canned water chestnuts rinse well. Leftover water chestnuts will keep in the refrigerator for several weeks if placed in a jar and covered with cold water. The water should be changed each day.

STIR-FRIED LAMB

500 g/1 lb lamb fillets, thinly sliced
1 tablespoon cornflour
2 tablespoons vegetable oil
3 onions, sliced
2 cloves garlic, crushed
2 tablespoons dry sherry
1 tablespoon soy sauce

1 Toss lamb in cornflour to coat. Heat 1 tablespoon oil in a wok or frying pan, add lamb and stir-fry for 4-5 minutes or until browned. Remove lamb from pan and set aside.

2 Heat remaining oil in pan, add onions and garlic and stir-fry for 5 minutes or until onions are soft. Stir in sherry and soy sauce, return lamb to pan and cook, stirring, for 2-3 minutes longer or until heated through.

Pork with Mushrooms

Serves 4

This recipe can be made using beef in place of the lamb if you wish.

VEGETARIAN

*Many of the most delicious vegetarian dishes eaten
in Western countries today have their origins in Asia. The
Chinese love vegetables, and those belonging to the Buddhist-
Taoist faith are vegetarians. A traditional Chinese meal
would include at least one or two vegetable dishes.*

Sweet and Sour Tofu

Spiced Potatoes
with Spinach

Hot and Sour
Thai Stir-Fry

Indonesian
Cooked Salad

Satay Stir-Fry

Coconut Vegetable
Stir-Fry

Sweet and Sour Tofu

52

SWEET AND SOUR TOFU

1 tablespoon peanut (groundnut) oil
250 g/8 oz tofu, cut into
2.5 cm/1 in cubes
1 red pepper, cut into thin strips
2 carrots, cut into thin strips
155 g/5 oz snow peas (mangetout)
2 teaspoons grated fresh ginger
1 clove garlic, crushed
315 g/10 oz canned pineapple pieces,
drained and juice reserved
1/3 cup/90 mL/3 fl oz water
1 tablespoon cornflour
1 tablespoon vinegar

1   Heat oil in a wok or frying pan, add tofu and stir-fry for 4-5 minutes or until golden. Remove tofu from pan and set aside.

2   Add red pepper, carrots, snow peas (mangetout), ginger and garlic to pan and stir-fry for 3 minutes.

3   Measure reserved pineapple juice to make up 1 cup/250 mL/8 fl oz – if there is insufficient juice, make up quantity with water. Combine pineapple juice, water, cornflour and vinegar, add to vegetable mixture and cook, stirring constantly, for 3-4 minutes or until sauce thickens and boils.

4   Add tofu and pineapple pieces to pan and cook for 2-3 minutes longer or until heated through.

Serves 4

Tofu or bean curd has been an important ingredient in Chinese and Japanese cuisines for over 1000 years. It has less than 5% fat, no cholesterol and virtually no sodium. Being extracted from soya beans, tofu is a good source of protein, minerals and B vitamins. It is also low in kilojoules (calories) with 75 g/2$^{1}/_{2}$ oz supplying only 200 kilojoules (48 calories).

SPICED POTATOES WITH SPINACH

90 g/3 oz butter
2 onions, sliced
4 tablespoons desiccated coconut
3 teaspoons grated fresh ginger
2 teaspoons ground turmeric
1 teaspoon yellow mustard seeds
1 teaspoon ground cumin
500 g/1 lb potatoes, diced
1 bunch/500 g/1 lb spinach, stalks
removed and leaves chopped
1/2 cup/125 mL/4 fl oz coconut milk
freshly ground black pepper

1   Melt butter in a frying pan, add onions and cook over a low heat, stirring frequently, for 10 minutes or until onions are soft and golden.

2   Add coconut and cook, stirring, for 3-4 minutes or until coconut is toasted. Stir in ginger, turmeric, mustard seeds and cumin and cook for 2-3 minutes longer.

3   Add potatoes to pan and stir to coat potatoes well with spice mixture. Cook over a medium heat, stirring frequently, for 10 minutes or until potatoes are just tender. Add spinach, coconut milk and black pepper to taste and cook for 4-5 minutes longer or until spinach wilts. Serve immediately.

Serves 6

Coconut milk can be purchased in a number of forms: canned, or as a long-life product in cartons, or as a powder to which you add water. Once opened it has a short life and should be used within a day or so. It is available from Asian food stores and some supermarkets.

HOT AND SOUR THAI STIR-FRY

2 tablespoons soy sauce
1 tablespoon dry sherry
1 fresh red chilli, seeded and
finely chopped
1 clove garlic, crushed
500 g/1 lb tofu, cubed and drained
1 tablespoon vegetable oil
2 onions, sliced
1 red pepper, cut into thin strips
1 green pepper, cut into thin strips
125 g/4 oz snow peas (mangetout)
125 g/4 oz egg noodles, cooked
and drained
2 spring onions, finely chopped
fresh coriander leaves to garnish

SPICY PEANUT SAUCE
2 cloves garlic, crushed
$^1/_2$ cup/125 g/4 oz crunchy
peanut butter
3 tablespoons lime or lemon juice
3 tablespoons soy sauce
1 small fresh red chilli, finely chopped
$^1/_2$ cup/125 mL/4 fl oz vegetable
stock or water

1   Place soy sauce, sherry, chilli and garlic in a bowl, and mix to combine. Add tofu, toss to coat and set aside to marinate for 30 minutes. Drain.

2   To make sauce, place garlic, peanut butter, lime or lemon juice, soy sauce and chilli in a food processor or blender and process to combine. With machine running, slowly add stock or water and process until combined.

3   Heat oil in a wok or frying pan, add onions and red and green peppers and stir-fry for 4-5 minutes or until vegetables start to soften. Remove onion mixture from pan and set aside. Add tofu to pan and stir-fry for 1-2 minutes. Return onion mixture to pan, add snow peas (mangetout) and noodles and stir-fry for 3-4 minutes longer. Stir in sauce and toss to coat all ingredients evenly. Transfer to a serving dish, garnish with spring onions and coriander leaves and serve immediately.

Serves 8

In Chinese culture noodles are a symbol of longevity and for this reason are usually served at Chinese New Year and birthday dinners. The Chinese believe that it is bad luck to cut noodles as it might shorten your life!

Left: Hot and Sour Thai Stir-Fry
Right: Indonesian Cooked Salad

INDONESIAN COOKED SALAD

2 potatoes, cut into chunks
4 carrots, sliced
250 g/8 oz green beans, sliced
$^1/_2$ bunch/250 g/8 oz spinach, stalks removed
2 tablespoons vegetable oil
125 g/4 oz bean sprouts
1 small cucumber, cut into sticks
1 large onion, sliced
2 hard-boiled eggs, quartered

PEANUT SAUCE
1 tablespoon vegetable oil
1 small onion, chopped
1 clove garlic, crushed
1 cup/250 mL/8 fl oz coconut milk
1 tablespoon lemon juice
5 tablespoons peanut butter
$^1/_2$ teaspoon chilli powder
1 bay leaf

1   Boil, steam or microwave potatoes, carrots, beans and spinach separately until just tender. Drain, place in a deep dish and toss to combine.

2   Heat 1 tablespoon oil in a wok or frying pan, add bean sprouts and cucumber and stir-fry for 2-3 minutes. Drain and sprinkle over vegetables in dish. Heat remaining oil in pan, add onion and stir-fry for 4-5 minutes or until golden. Drain and set aside.

3   To make sauce, heat oil in a saucepan, add onion and garlic and cook, stirring frequently, for 4-5 minutes or until onion is soft. Stir in coconut milk, lemon juice, peanut butter, chilli powder and bay leaf and cook, stirring constantly, for 4-5 minutes or until sauce thickens.

4   To serve, arrange eggs over vegetable mixture, pour over sauce and top with onions.

Serves 4

Poppadums are the perfect accompaniment to this unusual salad of lightly cooked vegetables topped with eggs and a spicy peanut sauce.

SATAY STIR-FRY

1 tablespoon vegetable oil
2 onions, cut into eighths
2 carrots, cut into thin strips
125 g/4 oz snow peas (mangetout),
sliced diagonally into 5 cm/2 in lengths
1 red pepper, cut into thin strips
1 bunch/500 g/1 lb spinach,
finely shredded
$^1/_2$ cup/125 mL/4 fl oz satay sauce
2 tablespoons chopped, roasted
unsalted peanuts

1   Heat oil in a wok or frying pan, add onions and stir-fry for 4-5 minutes or until soft.

2   Add carrots, snow peas (mangetout), red pepper and spinach to pan and stir-fry for 5 minutes or until vegetables are tender. Stir in satay sauce and peanuts and cook for 2-3 minutes or until heated through.

Serves 4

Prepared satay sauce is available from supermarkets and specialty food shops.

Coconut Vegetable Stir-Fry

2 tablespoons vegetable oil
2 carrots, cut into thin strips
125 g/4 oz green beans, chopped
1 stalk celery, diagonally sliced
1 onion, sliced
60 g/2 oz coconut chips or flakes
$^1/_2$ cup/125 mL/4 fl oz coconut milk
1 tablespoon Thai fish sauce
1-2 teaspoons chilli sauce, or to taste
1 tablespoon lime or lemon juice

1 Heat oil in a wok or frying pan, add carrots and stir-fry for 3 minutes. Add beans, celery and onion and stir-fry for 4-5 minutes longer or until vegetables are tender.

2 Add coconut chips or flakes, coconut milk, fish sauce, chilli sauce and lime or lemon juice and stir-fry for 3-4 minutes or until heated through.

Serves 4

Use any combination of vegetables that you have on hand to make this quick stir-fry. Adjust the vegetables you use according to the season and to suit your tastes.

SIDE DISHES

*Rice and noodles are an important part of any Asian
meal. In this chapter you will find delicious recipes for rice and
noodle dishes plus some interesting vegetable dishes that make
a great accompaniment to any meal.*

Indonesian Rice

58

INDONESIAN RICE

1¹/₂ cups/330 g/10¹/₂ oz basmati rice
2 tablespoons vegetable oil
2 onions, sliced
2 cloves garlic, crushed
2 teaspoons ground cumin
1 teaspoon ground coriander
2 teaspoons ground cardamom
2 fresh red chillies, chopped
2¹/₂ cups/600 mL/1 pt chicken stock
2 tablespoons honey
1 tablespoon soy sauce
2 spring onions, chopped

1   Place rice in a bowl, pour over enough hot water to cover and set aside to stand for 3 minutes. Drain.

2   Heat oil in a large frying pan, add onions and garlic and stir-fry for 4-5 minutes or until onion is soft. Add cumin, coriander, cardamom, chillies and rice and stir-fry for 1 minute. Combine stock, honey and soy sauce, stir into rice mixture and bring to the boil. Reduce heat and simmer for 10 minutes or until most of the liquid is absorbed.

3   Reduce heat to very low, cover and cook for 5 minutes longer or until all the liquid is absorbed. Stir in spring onions and serve immediately.

Serves 6

Basmati rice is an Oriental fragrant rice. Traditionally grown in the Himalayan foothills, basmati rice is used extensively in Indian cooking. Its name means 'fragrance' and you will notice its distinctive aroma as the rice cooks.

BRAISED BAMBOO SHOOTS

1 tablespoon vegetable oil
1 onion, sliced
1 red pepper, diced
440 g/14 oz canned bamboo shoots, drained and thinly sliced
1 tablespoon sesame seeds, toasted
1 tablespoon dry sherry
2 teaspoons soy sauce

1   Heat oil in a wok or frying pan, add onion and red pepper and stir-fry for 4-5 minutes or until onion is soft.

2   Add bamboo shoots, sesame seeds, sherry and soy sauce and stir-fry for 3-4 minutes longer or until heated through. Serve immediately.

Serves 4

Soy sauce is an essential ingredient in Asian cooking. The Chinese use two types of soy sauce – light soy sauce, labelled as Superior Soy, and dark soy sauce, labelled as Soy Superior Sauce. Generally, Western cooks prefer to use the light soy sauce – it is not as strong.

SESAME CABBAGE

1 tablespoon sesame oil
1 onion, chopped
60 g/2 oz bean sprouts
$^1/_2$ Chinese cabbage, chopped
2 fresh red chillies, chopped
$^1/_4$ cup/60 mL/2 fl oz water
freshly ground black pepper

The Chinese cabbage used in this recipe is widely available and looks rather like a tightly packed cos lettuce. It has firm, pale green, crinkled leaves. If it is not available, ordinary cabbage is also delicious prepared in this way.

1 Heat oil in a wok or frying pan, add onion and stir-fry for 4-5 minutes or until soft.

2 Add bean sprouts, cabbage, chillies and water and stir-fry for 4-5 minutes longer or until cabbage is tender. Season to taste with black pepper and serve immediately.

Serves 4

BRAISED GREEN VEGETABLES

2 tablespoons vegetable oil
1 tablespoon grated fresh ginger
2 onions, cut into wedges and separated
500 g/1 lb broccoli, broken into florets
4 stalks celery, diagonally sliced
6 stalks English spinach, chopped
250 g/8 oz snow peas (mangetout)
$^3/_4$ cup/185 mL/6 fl oz chicken stock
freshly ground black pepper
8 spring onions, diagonally sliced

1 Heat oil in a wok or frying pan, add ginger and onions and stir-fry for 2-3 minutes. Add broccoli and celery and stir-fry for 2-3 minutes longer.

2 Add spinach and snow peas (mangetout) and stir-fry for 2-3 minutes. Stir in chicken stock and bring to the boil. Reduce heat, cover pan and simmer 4-5 minutes or until vegetables are just tender. Add spring onions and serve immediately.

Serves 6

Sesame Cabbage,
Garlic Beans

GARLIC BEANS

1 cup/250 mL/8 fl oz chicken stock
250 g/8 oz green beans
1 tablespoon vegetable oil
2 cloves garlic, crushed
4 spring onions, diagonally sliced
2 teaspoons soy sauce
1 teaspoon sesame oil

1   Place stock in a saucepan and bring to the boil. Add beans and cook for 10 minutes or until tender. Drain and refresh under cold running water.

2   Heat vegetable oil in a wok or frying pan, add garlic and spring onions and stir-fry for 1 minute. Add beans, soy sauce and sesame oil and stir-fry for 2-3 minutes or until heated through. Serve immediately.

Serves 4

To clean a wok, wash with water (do not use detergent), then dry thoroughly. The best way to dry the wok is to place it over a low heat for a few minutes.

FRIED BROWN RICE

1¹/₂ cups/330 g/10¹/₂ oz brown rice
2 tablespoons peanut (groundnut) oil
2 stalks celery, chopped
1 red pepper, chopped
2 cloves garlic, crushed
2 eggs, lightly beaten
60 g/2 oz peas, cooked
4 spring onions, chopped
1 tablespoon soy sauce

While not traditional – the Chinese do not use brown rice – this version of fried rice is delicious. You can, of course, use white rice if you prefer.

1   Cook rice in boiling water until tender. Drain, spread out on a tray and refrigerate until cold.

2   Heat oil in a wok or frying pan, add celery, red pepper and garlic and stir-fry for 4-5 minutes or until vegetables are just tender. Remove vegetables from pan and set aside.

3   Pour eggs into pan and cook over a low heat, stirring, until eggs are set. Chop roughly and set aside.

4   Add rice to pan and stir-fry to separate grains. Return vegetable mixture and eggs to pan, add peas, spring onions and soy sauce and stir-fry for 3-4 minutes or until heated through.

Serves 4

COLD SPICY NOODLES

500 g/1 lb egg noodles
2 teaspoons sesame oil
6 spring onions, finely chopped

SPICY SAUCE
3 tablespoons sesame paste
¹/₂ teaspoon chilli powder or to taste
2 cloves garlic, finely chopped
2 tablespoons soy sauce
1 teaspoon sugar

Noodles are an important staple in northern China where it is too cold for rice to grow.
This noodle dish is served cold and is delicious in a packed lunch or to take on a picnic.

1   Cook noodles in boiling water in a large saucepan following packet directions. Drain, rinse under cold running water, drain again and set aside to cool completely.

2   To make sauce, place sesame paste, chilli powder, garlic, soy sauce and sugar in a food processor or blender and process to combine.

3   Toss cold noodles in sesame oil, place in a serving bowl, top with sauce, toss well to combine, then sprinkle with spring onions.

Serves 6

Fried Brown Rice

DESSERTS

*While the Chinese enjoy sweet dishes they are seldom
served at the end of a meal as in Western cultures. The most
popular finish to a meal would be fresh seasonal fruit. The
recipes in this chapter are light and refreshing and make the
perfect finish to a Chinese or Asian-style meal.*

Custard Tarts

Sesame Toffee Apples

Mandarin and Lychee
Mousse

Fruit with Coconut
Custard

Custard Tarts

CUSTARD TARTS

375 g/12 oz prepared shortcrust pastry
$^1/_2$ cup/125 g/4 oz sugar
$^3/_4$ cup/185 mL/6 fl oz water
3 eggs, lightly beaten
$^1/_3$ cup/90 mL/3 fl oz milk

1   Roll out pastry to 3 mm/$^1/_8$ in thick and, using an 8 cm/3$^1/_4$ in cutter, cut out 24 circles. Press pastry circles into lightly greased shallow patty tins (tartlet tins).

2   Place sugar and water in a saucepan and cook over a medium heat without boiling, stirring constantly until sugar is dissolved. Remove pan from heat and set aside to cool.

3   Add eggs and milk to sugar syrup and mix to combine. Pour egg mixture into pastry cases and bake for 10 minutes, then reduce oven temperature to 180°C/350°F/ Gas 4 and cook for 10 minutes longer or until custard is set.

Makes 24 tarts

Oven temperature
200°C, 400°F, Gas 6

Custard tarts appear on many Yum Cha menus. They are not only delicious, but also surprisingly easy to make.

SESAME TOFFEE APPLES

6 apples, cored, peeled and quartered
$^1/_4$ cup/30 g/1 oz flour
1 tablespoon cornflour
2 egg whites
vegetable oil for deep-frying

SESAME TOFFEE
1 cup/250 g/8 oz sugar
$^1/_3$ cup/90 mL/3 fl oz water
1 tablespoon sesame seeds

1   Dust apples with a little of the flour. Place remaining flour and cornflour in a bowl, stir in egg whites and mix to make a smooth batter.

2   Heat oil in a deep saucepan until a cube of bread browns in 50 seconds. Dip apple pieces in batter and cook a few at a time in oil until golden. Drain on absorbent kitchen paper.

3   To make toffee, place sugar and water in a saucepan and cook over a medium heat, stirring constantly, without boiling, until sugar is dissolved. Bring sugar syrup to the boil, without stirring, and cook until syrup turns a light golden colour. Remove pan from heat and stir in sesame seeds.

4   Dip apple pieces into hot syrup then drop into a bowl of iced water to set the toffee. Serve warm.

Serves 6

While this dish takes a little time to prepare and cook, it is well worth the effort. Other fruits, such as bananas and oranges, are also delicious cooked in this way.

*Right: Mandarin and
Lychee Mousse
Far right: Fruit with
Coconut Custard*

MANDARIN AND LYCHEE MOUSSE

315 g/10 oz canned mandarin segments,
drained and $^1/4$ cup/60 mL/2 fl oz
juice reserved
440 g/14 oz canned lychees, drained and
$^1/2$ cup/125 mL/4 fl oz juice reserved
3 teaspoons gelatine
$^1/2$ cup/125 mL/4 fl oz cream (double)
$^1/2$ cup/125 g/4 oz sour cream

1   Place reserved mandarin and lychee juices in a heatproof bowl, set over a saucepan of simmering water, sprinkle gelatine over juices and cook, stirring frequently, for 10 minutes or until gelatine dissolves. Remove from heat and set aside to cool.

2   Place mandarins and lychees in a food processor or blender and process until smooth. Transfer fruit pureé to a bowl, stir in gelatine mixture, cream and sour cream and mix well to combine. Spoon mousse into serving glasses and refrigerate until set.

Serves 4

Lychees are native to southern China and are the fruit of the litchi tree. They are a small, delicately flavoured fruit with a white flesh and tough brown skin.

FRUIT WITH COCONUT CUSTARD

1 small pineapple, sliced
250 g/8 oz strawberries
¹/₂ rockmelon (cantaloupe), sliced
2 kiwifruit, sliced

COCONUT CUSTARD
4 eggs
¹/₃ cup/90 g/3 oz sugar
1 cup/250 mL/8 fl oz coconut milk
1 cup/250 mL/8 fl oz milk

1   To make custard, place eggs and sugar in a heatproof bowl and beat until thick and creamy. Add coconut milk and milk. Place bowl over a saucepan of simmering water and cook, stirring constantly, until custard thickens.

2   Arrange fruit attractively on serving plates, spoon custard over fruit and serve immediately.

Serves 6

Don't keep this dessert just for an Asian-style meal.

SESAME PRAWN TOASTS

185 g/6 oz uncooked prawns,
shelled and deveined
1 teaspoon grated fresh ginger
1 clove garlic, crushed
2 teaspoons cornflour
1 egg white
$1/8$ teaspoon five spice powder
freshly ground black pepper
4 thin slices white bread, crusts removed
3 tablespoons sesame seeds
vegetable oil for shallow-frying

2 Place egg white in a bowl and whisk with a fork until frothy. Stir egg white into prawn mixture. Add five spice powder and season to taste with black pepper.

1 Place prawns, ginger, garlic and cornflour in a food processor and process to mince prawns.

3 Press prawn mixture evenly and firmly onto bread slices. Sprinkle with sesame seeds and press firmly. Heat 2 cm/$3/4$ in oil in a large frying pan. Place prawn-covered bread, prawn side down in hot oil and fry for 2-3 minutes or until golden. To keep bread slices immersed during cooking, hold down with a fish slice. Remove prawn toasts from oil, drain on absorbent kitchen paper, cut into fingers and serve immediately.

Serves 4

CHINESE DUMPLINGS

250 g/8 oz canned bamboo shoots,
drained
4 spring onions
250 g/8 oz lean pork mince
$^1/_2$ teaspoon grated fresh ginger
1 egg white
2 teaspoons soy sauce
20 wonton or spring roll wrappers,
each 12.5 cm/5 in square

3   Place a teaspoon of pork mixture in the centre of each wrapper. Bring wrapper up around filling and squeeze to make a money bag shape. Place dumplings in a bamboo steamer, set over boiling water and steam for 20 minutes.

When not using wonton or spring roll wrappers keep them covered with a damp teatowel to prevent them drying out and cracking.

Makes 20

1   Finely chop bamboo shoots and spring onions.

For even cooking make sure that the dumplings are not touching when you place them in the steamer.

2   Place bamboo shoots, spring onions, pork, ginger, egg white and soy sauce in a bowl and mix to combine.

NASI GORENG

1 cup/220 g/7 oz long grain rice
3 tablespoons vegetable oil
2 onions, sliced
2 cloves garlic, crushed
2 small fresh green chillies, seeded
and chopped
185 g/6 oz pork fillet, diced
185 g/6 oz boneless chicken breast
fillets, diced
$^1/_4$ teaspoon chilli powder
1 teaspoon paprika
2 tablespoons soy sauce
250 g/8 oz cooked prawns,
shelled and deveined
1 egg
1 teaspoon water
15 g/$^1/_2$ oz butter

2   Heat oil in a wok or frying pan, add onions, garlic and chillies and stir-fry for 2 minutes. Add pork and chicken and stir-fry for 10 minutes or until cooked. Add chilli powder, paprika, soy sauce, prawns and rice and stir-fry for 5-6 minutes longer or until heated through. Transfer rice mixture to a serving dish and keep warm.

1   Cook rice in boiling water for 12 minutes or until tender. Drain, rinse well and drain again.

A heavy wok made of carbon steel will give better cooking results than the lighter stainless steel or aluminium woks.

'A long-handled metal spatula or spoon is the ideal cooking implement for stir-frying food in a wok.'

3 Place egg and water in a bowl and whisk to combine. Melt butter in a small frying pan, add egg mixture and swirl pan to give a thin layer. Cook over a low heat for 2-3 minutes or until set and golden on the base. Turn omelette onto a board, roll up and cut into slices. Place omelette slices on rice mixture and serve immediately.

Serves 4

CHINESE FRIED RICE

2 tablespoons vegetable oil
6 spring onions, chopped
125 g/4 oz mushrooms, chopped
$^1/_2$ red pepper, chopped
$^1/_2$ green pepper, chopped
1 cup/220 g/7 oz long grain rice,
cooked and cooled
250 g/8 oz cooked prawns,
shelled and deveined
125 g/4 oz ham, diced
$^1/_2$ teaspoon ground ginger
$^1/_4$ teaspoon cayenne pepper

3 Add prawns, ham, ginger and cayenne pepper and stir-fry for 3-4 minutes longer or until heated through.

One of the easiest ways to cook rice for fried rice is to cook it in the microwave. To cook rice in the microwave, place 1 cup/220 g/7 oz rice and 2 cups/500 mL/16 fl oz water in a large microwave-safe container. Cook uncovered on HIGH (100%) for 12-15 minutes or until liquid is absorbed. Cover and stand for 5 minutes. Toss with a fork and use as required.

1 Heat oil in a wok or frying pan, add spring onions, mushrooms and red and green pepper and stir-fry for 2-3 minutes.

2 Add rice and stir-fry for 3 minutes longer.

Serves 4

NOODLE BRUSHES

1 For each brush you will need 15 sticks of somen noodles and a strip of nori seaweed.

2 Break ends off noodles, to make lengths of about 10 cm/4 in. Cut a strip of nori and wrap around middle of each bundle of noodles. Moisten ends of nori strip with a little egg white so that it sticks together. Set aside to stand for a few minutes to allow the nori to dry.

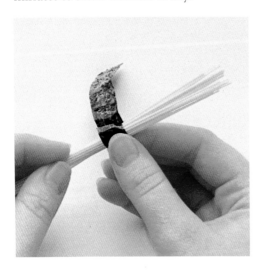

3 Cut through the middle of each nori strip to make two brushes. Heat oil in a large saucepan, until a cube of bread browns in 50 seconds. Add noodle bundles to hot oil and cook for about 30 seconds or until noodles spread and are golden. Remove from oil and drain on absorbent kitchen paper.

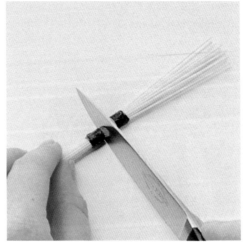

The fine wheat noodles from Japan called somen noodles are used to make these deep-fried brushes which are used to garnish fried foods. They are fun to make and pleasant to eat.

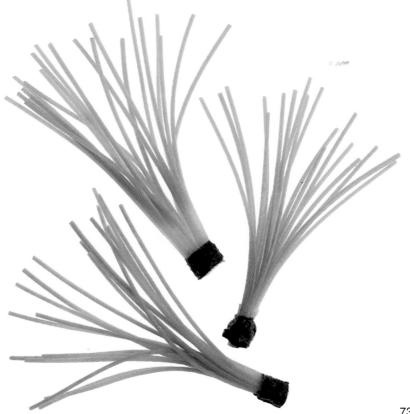

EGG AND NORI ROLLS

3 eggs
1 tablespoon cold water
2 sheets nori seaweed

1   Place eggs and water in a bowl and beat to combine. Set aside.

2   Toast nori sheets by holding over gas flame or an electric hotplate set on a medium heat. When toasting nori take care that it does not burn.

Nori is one of six types of edible seaweed harvested by the Japanese. Nori is available from Asian food stores.

3   Reserve 1 tablespoon egg mixture. Pour a quarter of remaining egg mixture into a greased frying pan and cook, on one side only, until set. Remove omelette from pan and set aside. Repeat with remaining mixture to make four omelettes.

4   Place an omelette, uncooked side up, on a bamboo mat, top with nori cut to fit, then another omelette, repeating layers until all omelettes and nori are used. Using the mat as a guide, roll up and seal edges with reserved egg mixture. Set aside until cold, then remove mat and cut into slices.

Makes 8

PRAWN CRISPS

Prawn crisps are available from Asian food stores and some supermarkets.

To cook, heat oil in a large saucepan to moderately hot. To test, drop a prawn crisp into the oil; it should puff up and float to the surface almost immediately. Cook a few crisps at a time and remove as soon as they come to the surface. Drain on absorbent kitchen paper. Serve immediately or allow to cool and store in an airtight container until required.

Prawn crisps can also be cooked in the microwave – this is a no-fat way of cooking. To cook in the microwave, place crisps on absorbent kitchen paper and cook on HIGH (100%) until crisps puff up.

USING CHOPSTICKS

The traditional eating utensil of China and some other Asian countries is chopsticks. With a little practise and know-how these at first awkward looking sticks are in fact quite easy to use. Follow these easy instructions and learn how to use chopsticks correctly.

1   Place one chopstick in your right hand. Holding it with the base of your thumb and the top of your forefinger, with your fingers slightly bent.

2   Hold the second chopstick by the top of your thumb and the tops of your middle and index fingers.

3   While eating, the bottom chopstick remains stationary and the top one is moved up and down by the middle and index fingers to pick up the food.

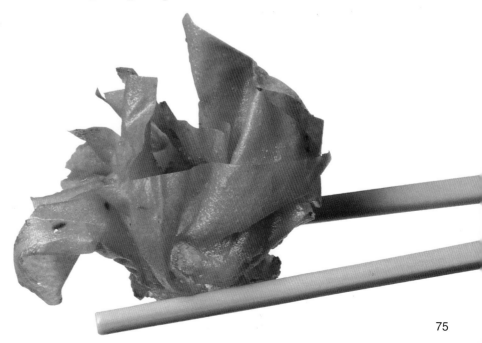

ASIAN INGREDIENTS

BAMBOO SHOOTS: These are the young edible shoots of certain kinds of bamboo. Available, canned, from Asian food stores and some supermarkets, they are pale yellow in colour and have a crunchy texture.

BLACK BEANS: Also known as salted black beans, these are small black soy beans. Their unique flavour is achieved by fermenting them with salt and spices. They have a slightly salty taste and a rich smell, and are usually used as a seasoning. Available, canned, from Asian food stores. If leftover beans are stored in an airtight container in the refrigerator they will keep indefinitely.

CHILLI PASTE (sambal oelek): This is a paste of chillies and salt that can be used as an ingredient or condiment.

CHILLI SAUCE: Chinese chilli sauce is a bright red, hot sauce made from chillies, vinegar, sugar and salt. Sometimes used in cooking, it is most popular as a dipping sauce for foods such as spring rolls and wontons. For those who find this sauce too strong, try diluting it with a little hot water.

CHINESE DRIED MUSHROOMS: These are fairly expensive, but a few will add a unique flavour to any dish. To use dried mushrooms, place mushrooms in a bowl, cover with hot water and set aside to soak for about 20 minutes or until soft. Squeeze out excess liquid, remove tough stem and use as required. For added flavour, the soaking liquid is often added to dishes.

FIVE SPICE POWDER: This pungent, fragrant, spicy and slightly sweet powder is a mixture of star anise, Szechuan peppercorns, fennel, cloves and cinnamon.

EGG NOODLES: The flat Oriental noodles are often used in soups, while the round noodles are served with sauces and are best for stir-fries. They are also served as an accompaniment, instead of rice.

FISH SAUCE: This is the drained liquid from salted fermented anchovies. It is an essential ingredient in Thai and Vietnamese cooking.

GLUTINOUS RICE: This round-grained rice is used for stuffings and desserts. If it is unavailable, short-grain or pudding rice can be used in its place.

HOISIN SAUCE: Also known as Chinese barbecue sauce, this is a thick, dark brown sauce made from soy beans, vinegar, sugar, spices and other flavourings. It has a sweet spicy flavour and is mainly used in southern Chinese cooking.

LOTUS ROOT: In India and China the lotus plant is considered to be sacred. Lotus root, as the name suggests, is the root of the lotus plant and is perforated with holes. It is used extensively as a garnish in Chinese and Japanese cooking. It is available canned or dried. When using dried lotus root, first soak it in hot water with $1/2$ teaspoon lemon juice for 20 minutes.

OYSTER SAUCE: Made from a concentrate of oysters cooked in soy sauce and brine, oyster sauce is dark brown in colour and has a rich flavour. It is used both in cooking and as a condiment.

PLUM SAUCE: A popular dipping sauce, plum sauce is made from plums preserved in vinegar, sugar, chillies and spices.

RICE NOODLES: Also called rice vermicelli or rice sticks, these noodles vary in size from a narrow vermicelli style

There are many varieties of dried Chinese mushrooms. They are fairly expensive but keep indefinitely and add a distinctive flavour and aroma to many Chinese dishes. Store dried mushrooms in an airtight container.

to a ribbon noodle about 5 mm wide. Made from rice flour, these noodles are served with spicy sauces and used in soups and stir-fry dishes. The noodles should be soaked before using; the narrow noodles require about 10 minutes soaking, while the wider ones will need about 30 minutes. These noodles are sometimes deep-fried in which case there is no need to soak them. When fried they puff up and become crisp.

SESAME SEED OIL: This strongly flavoured oil is used as a seasoning and is made from roasted sesame seeds. Usually added at the end of cooking. It is available from Asian food shops and keeps indefinitely.

SESAME PASTE: Made from sesame seeds, this is a rich, thick creamy-coloured paste that is popular in the cooking of north and west China. If it is unavailable you can use peanut butter in its place.

SOY SAUCE: An essential ingredient for Chinese cooking. Soy sauce is made by fermenting soy beans with flour and water. It is then aged and distilled to make the resulting sauce. There are two types of soy sauce – light and dark. The Chinese use light soy sauce for cooking. In Chinese food stores it is labelled Superior Soy. Dark soy sauce is aged for longer than the light one, is slightly thicker and has a stronger flavour. The Chinese prefer to use this sauce as a dipping sauce and for stews. In Chinese food stores it is labelled Soy Superior Sauce.

STRAW MUSHROOMS: These are available canned from Asian food stores. Before using, drain and rinse well.

TOFU: Also known as bean curd, tofu has played an important role in Chinese cooking for over a thousand years. It is

made from yellow soy beans which are soaked, ground and mixed with water then briefly cooked before being solidified. It is rich in protein yet low in fat and cholesterol free.

TRANSPARENT NOODLES: Also called cellophane noodles, these noodles are added to Oriental soups and deep-fried as a garnish.

WATER CHESTNUTS: White, crunchy and about the size of a walnut, water chestnuts are a sweet root vegetable. Canned water chestnuts are available from Chinese food stores and some supermarkets. In China, fresh water chestnuts are boiled in their skins, then peeled and simmered with rock sugar and eaten as a snack. They are also popular in cooked dishes. When using canned water chestnuts rinse them well first.

WONTON WRAPPERS: These paper-thin pastry wrappers are available from Chinese food stores and some supermarkets.

INDEX

Acknowledgments

The publisher wishes to thank the following companies for their continuing support.

Admiral Appliances

Black & Decker
(Australasia) Pty Ltd

Blanco Appliances

Around food, only
GLAD is good enough

Master Foods the
Taste Masters

Meadow Lea Foods

Namco Cookware

Ricegrowers Co-op
Mills Ltd

Tycraft Pty Ltd,
distributors of Braun

White Wings Foods
for Better Baking

Published by Grange Books
an imprint of Grange Books Plc
The Grange
Kingsnorth Industrial Estate
Hoo, nr Rochester
Kent ME3 9ND
www.Grangebooks.co.uk
Copyright © Trident Press International 2002

Quick & Easy Chinese & Oriental Cooking

Recipe Development: Sheryle Eastwood, Lucy Kelly, Donna Hay,
Anneka Mitchell, Penelope Peel, Belinda Warn, Loukie Werle
Photography: Simon Butcher, Paul Grater, Per Ericson, Ashley Mackevicius,
Harm Mol, Yanto Noerianto, Andy Payne, Warren Webb
Styling: Wendy Berecry, Belinda Clayton, Rosemary De Santis,
Carolyn Fienberg, Jacqui Hing, Michelle Gorry
Cover Photography: Garry Smith
Cover Styling: Janet Lodge
Cover Design: Paul Sims

Includes Index
ISBN 1-84013-480-1
EAN 9781840134803

This Edition 2002

Printed in China